For Those Seeking

Addiction Is A Family Disease

Art Diel (signature)

COMPILED AND WRITTEN BY ART DIELHENN
COVER AND BOOK ILLUSTRATIONS BY CLEMMY MCWILLIAM-LE BUSQUE
FOREWORD BY DR. WARREN "BEAU" CHRISTIANSON, ADDICTION PSYCHIATRIST

media contact : John Stellar
tel: 818-853-7100   john@e-pr.com

For those who keep coming back

First published by Ultimate World Publishing 2024
Copyright © 2024 Arthur B. Dielhenn

ISBN

Paperback: 978-1-923255-46-3
Ebook: 978-1-923255-47-0

Arthur B. Dielhenn has asserted his rights under the Copyright, Designs and Patents Act 1988 to be identified as the author of this work. The information in this book is based on the author's experiences and opinions. The publisher specifically disclaims responsibility for any adverse consequences which may result from use of the information contained herein. Permission to use information has been sought by the author. Any breaches will be rectified in further editions of the book.

All rights reserved. No part of this publication may be reproduced, stored in or introduced into a retrieval system, or transmitted in any form, or by any means (electronic, mechanical, photocopying, recording or otherwise) without the prior written permission of the author. Any person who does any unauthorized act in relation to this publication may be liable to criminal prosecution and civil claims for damages. Enquiries should be made through the publisher.

Cover design: Ultimate World Publishing
Cover Illustration: Clemmy Le Busque
Layout and typesetting: Ultimate World Publishing
Editors: Marnae Kelly, Larry Gerber, Maureen Grady, Kat Chezum

Ultimate World Publishing
Diamond Creek,
Victoria Australia 3089
www.writeabook.com.au

The Stuff Inside

RESULTS STUFF

Foreword

My name is Dr. Warren Christianson. I am an addiction psychiatrist.

I should begin by saying that I am biased when it comes to the author of this book. Truth is, I am a huge fan. Art helped me in his capacity as a career coach when I was fresh out of training and starting my career as a director of the chemical dependence program in Pasadena, California. I still work there today.

My approach to addiction work with patients starts with a thorough life history. It is a rare thing for a person to methodically march through time starting from birth, through the important moments, to finally arrive in the present. Things become clearer as this history unfolds. It's a powerful thing to tell this story, to have it heard, acknowledged, and appreciated by a stranger, albeit a psychiatrist.

In this process we pay special attention to the patient's family: parents, grandparents, siblings, stepparents, and anybody else who was part of the tribe.

How did everybody get along? What did they do? Who were the family heroes? Who were the villains? What were the difficulties faced? Were addiction issues present, either clearly or hidden? If you were grading your family members, what letter grade would you give them? What grade would they give themselves? What grade would you give yourself?

The early stuff matters. It provides the template—the road map—for how we think we are supposed to live, what we are supposed to run from or chase after, what we are supposed to accomplish. The list goes on and on. Our early identity, the very notion of "ME," comes from our early experiences. This is where we start to form the myth of who we are.

This can be wonderful news if we grew up hearing a "good story" about who we are and how the world works. But what if we were told a misleading story about how the world works or who we are? What if we were told we are worthless and felt that we had no place in this world? What if we experienced trauma? What if dysfunction ruled our early years, causing harm, pain, and confusion? What if one of the ways we tried to cope was to escape it all? What if addiction became a part of our story?

Then perhaps, in later years, recovery would also become part of our story.

Luckily, in recovery, we get the chance to reexamine ourselves, our families, and the stories cemented into our history. With this reexamination, we learn to accept our past behaviors, our family dysfunction, and our emotional response to all of it. In doing this important work we open the way to choosing a new way forward.

In our chemical dependence program, we have found Art's first book, *Get Out Of Your Head, It's A Mess In There!* to be particularly useful as a thought-provoking starting point for group discussions. In this book, the focus is on how we talk to ourselves about our stories and the emotional ruts we fall into as a result of this self-talk. It then goes on to suggest ways to manage and replace this looping narrative.

We will utilize his new book, *Addiction Is A Family Disease*, in a similar way. But this time with the emphasis on how family life plays a pivotal role in identity formation and subsequent addiction challenges. That's only the beginning. The rest focuses on many critical tools of recovery and the benefits of committing to them.

Though we use his books in a clinical setting, they are not clinical books. It's one man's journey through recovery that is not only representative of his experience but resonates universally. It's simple and easily accessible, and Clemmy's cartoons lighten the mood.

Addiction is comforting in a way, with its chronic compulsive sameness. Recovery can be uncomfortable in its newness, freedom, and lightness. The same is true of our families. They can be the rock that we stand on or the avalanche that buries us. But they made us who we are, in all our miraculous imperfection! Let's read this book with an eye towards questioning, amending, accepting, and honoring all our various parts then get out there and start walking the wild, liberating path of recovery!

Warren "Beau" Christianson, D.O.
Director of Aurora Las Encinas Hospital
Chemical Dependency Services
Adjunct Professor of Psychiatry USC/Keck Medical School

"I'm tired of living in my own shadow, of being a slave to my addictions, my ambitions, my weaknesses."
— **Mia Asher**

CHAPTER 1

Why I Wrote This Book

Addiction in any form is a monumental challenge for sufferers, their families, friends, and employers. I have been in recovery for a while now and meeting that challenge has transformed my experience in life.

I wrote this book to stay vigilant in my own recovery and as a reminder of the gifts I've been given.

It seems to me that we are all recovering from something almost all the time. It's not just addicts and their loved ones— it's all of us! We all have challenges and injuries, physical and mental. We all have bad days, make mistakes, and bounce back.

Recovery is a life process as normal as waking in the morning or turning in at night. It's the process that allows us to regain our center, find our strength, and move forward.

A runner pulls a hamstring. Recovery is critical before she runs again. A couple divorces. How do they mend? A dear friend dies … a tornado strikes. How do we deal?

We grieve, we rebuild, and we recover.

I have had to recover from many things: a broken home, difficult parents, dyslexia, failure in school, divorce, the death of a child, spiritual disconnection …

Oh, and bad hair days, nightmares, sleep deprivation, a kitchen renovation, writing this book, parking tickets, accidents, mistakes, miscalculations, pimples, weight gain, aches, pains, and a big nose.

I am even trying to recover from old age, with diminishing success.

Many of these ups and downs are out of our control, and some are of our own making. We must show up and recover from all of them to move on and enjoy the life we have.

The world is constantly recovering from illness, hatred, insanity, aggression, climate change, war, colossal amounts of stupidity, entitlement, ignorance, denial, floods, famine, and the pillaging of the very earth that sustains us.

We are all affected, one way or another, all the time. Our instinct is to redo, reboot, recover again and again, and carry on.

There are many words in our language that refer to this process of renewal. Certainly, it must be important.

Recover

RehabilitateRestorRenewReorganizeRebuildReconstruct
ReestablishRefurbishReplaceReinforceReinstateRenovate
RepairRevitalizeRefreshRecallReconditionReconstitute
ReintroduceRejuvenateReviveReviewRecalibrateRegain
RedeemRedirectRenewReassureRebirthReboundRebuke
RechargeReclaimReconsiderRecreateRedesignReelect
ReformRefurbishRegainRegenerateReinvigorateReimburse
ReinforceRemakeRemarryReassembleRememberRemodel
ReopenRescheduleResettleRestoreRestructureReunify
ReabsorbReaccomodateReacquaintReacquireReact
ReactivateReadaptReadjustReadmitReadministerReadmit
ReaffirmReaffixReaggrigateReallocateRealignReanalyse

ReanimateReappearReappointRehydrateReapportion ReappointRefreezeReaffixRecheckReabsorb...RE.... Everything.

YIKES! A lot of words for do-overs. And there are hundreds more.

It's in choosing recovery and restoration that we face our frailty, overcome our fear, and decide to embrace the bounty of life's sacred geometry.

———

Being in recovery is a subset of *recovering from*. Being in recovery means something quite specific: an opportunity to deal with more extreme issues—addictions and behaviors that can be harmful, debilitating, and even fatal.

I have been addicted to a bunch of stuff during my lifetime: TV, sugar, nicotine, alcohol, anger, control, denial, work, co-dependence, lust, self-pity, and isolation, to name a few.

I used to obsess and worry, ruminating on stupid thoughts endlessly. It was hard to turn off the TV as a kid because I would rather escape into illusion than face the realities of my actual life.

I have been able to kick or modify many of these tendencies, but chocolate fudge brownie ice cream and double chocolate chip cookies are still hard to resist. I think about them a lot, much like I used to think about the cocktail hour . . . or two . . . or three.

TV, sugar, nicotine, alcohol, anger, control, denial, work...

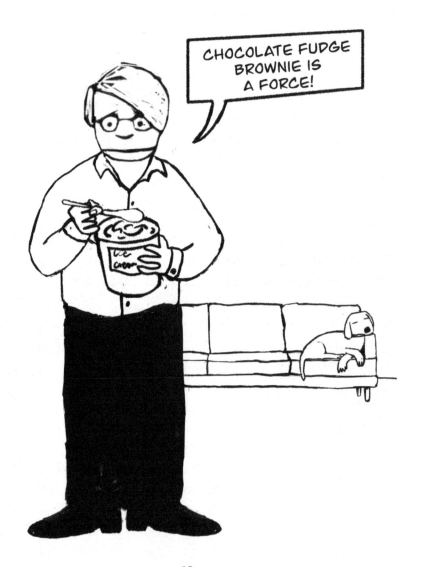

I have loved ones and friends with substance and behavioral issues. Addiction is often passed down, bequeathed to successive generations.

The addict may be the obvious problem, but family and friends are also deeply affected. Family relations and reactions to the addict's behaviors can become addictive and obsessive, making those folks sick too.

No one is spared addiction's wrath—like an emotional, physical, and spiritual tsunami, it threatens everyone in its path.

Addiction is a family disease.

———

Addicts and co-dependent loved ones are a perfect fit. The addict *needs to be rescued,* and the loved one is *compelled to rescue.* Rescuers, serious about their purpose, often attract easygoing, fun-loving addicts.

The two are like puzzle pieces fitting snugly together. As time trudges on, the rescuer is martyred by the insanity of the disease and slowly becomes just another victim.

Many of us caught in these repetitive spirals are not even aware that we are stuck. We may think it's normal because we've been held in their grip for so long.

I empathize. I've been there and continue to work on mitigating these habits myself. They are sneaky. They resist change.

Tread lightly. Approach what follows with kindness and care for yourself and others. None of this is easy. Unaware, many of us fall victim through no fault of our own, but it happens, nonetheless.

————

We hear much about addiction, much about how difficult recovery is, and how few commit to the process. Statistically speaking, the numbers are not in our favor. It takes real fortitude and a fierceness of purpose to choose recovery. Some of us come willingly and some kicking and screaming, but all who remain seek a gentler more harmonious life, and those who don't may find that things just keep getting worse.

We have seen this on TV and in movies, mass media, and perhaps even our or others' life experiences. What we don't hear much about is the joy of recovery. We don't hear much about this rebirth into the wonder of once again living a purposeful, fulfilling life. It's a miracle.

We learn to laugh again, love again, to be productive community members again. We develop a higher degree of consciousness, awareness, and acceptance. We stop taking everything personally, most of the time at least. We make amends for damage done to others; we commit to changing our ways.

The changes can be deeply enriching—breathtaking even, propelled by the human spirit's desire to sustain itself and thrive. As a recovering friend says, "It's like watching your dog talk!"

"It's a miracle. It's like watching your dog talk."

————

I am deeply indebted to the recovery programs I practice. I am passing on much of what I have learned from the wisdom of others.

Though I have gathered, synthesized, and referenced much from these programs, this book is not affiliated with them in any way and should not be taken as a discussion of any particular recovery program.

This book is about my experience in recovery. I am only one among many.

There is a very high correlation between addiction and mental illness. If you have a family member or friend suffering from both, then recovery can be doubly challenging. This book is no substitute for professional care.

Can you imagine a life free of addiction?

CHAPTER 2

Why Read This Book

I didn't set out to have addiction issues. When I was five, sitting in the bathtub, playing with my cereal-box frogman, I didn't say to myself, "Gosh, when I grow up, I think I'll be a lying, cheating, drunken bum swilling pints of rotgut from a paper bag!"

Hell no! I wanted to be an FBI frogman. I was going to save the world. Nobody sets out to be an addict.

Genes can predispose us to addiction. So can family circumstances. Traumatized children and children of alcoholic parents and relatives are at risk.

Some people's body and brain chemistry fail to process alcohol and drugs. Once they start using, they need more to manage the mental compulsion and physical symptoms of withdrawal.

There is escape in indulging in drugs, alcohol, food, gambling, shopping, love, sex, co-dependence, work, pornography, social media, video games, cell phones...

In moderation, these little escapes make sense: a nip of brandy against the chill, comfort food when upset, shopping to get out of the house, a lottery ticket to fantasize a financial windfall, a trip to Vegas, giving advice to someone who needs our help. Why not?

That said, indulged repetitively, time after time, these little escapes can evolve into repetitive habits that can eventually create bigger problems than the problems they were meant to relieve. They can launch us into self-destructive trends. Once hooked, it's hard to get free.

Though the severity of addictions varies widely, most are progressive, building over time. In addicts, compulsions are always there, sometimes obvious, sometimes not.

Many of us with these tendencies often play *Whack-A-Mole* with several conditions and layers of distortion. As we beat one down, others pop up. The addictive personality is like Wile E. Coyote and won't be denied.

————

In his book *How Not to Kill Yourself*, Clancy Martin suggests that "Thinking about killing oneself and addictive thinking have a lot more in common than is normally recognized. Wanting to kill yourself is like an extreme version of the relief you find after drinking a few glasses of wine."

Why are some of us so bent on self-destruction? Because the "psychache" we are experiencing is so profound and debilitating that any escape seems like the better option.

Edwin Shneidman, co-founder of the Los Angeles Suicide Prevention Center, coined "psychache" to indicate an unbearable inner anguish that can lead to suicide if left unresolved.

Dr. William D. Silkworth, the pioneer of alcoholism research, said the disease combined "an obsession of the mind that condemns one to drink and an allergy of the body that condemns one to die."

The American Society of Addiction Medicine defines addiction as "A treatable, chronic medical disease involving complex interactions among brain circuits, genetics, the environment, and an individual's life experiences. People with addiction use substances or engage in behaviors that become compulsive and often continue despite harmful consequences. Prevention efforts and treatment approaches for addiction are generally as successful as those for other chronic diseases."

If I don't treat my disease, It will treat me.

It's easier to understand and manage an addiction when we understand the underlying conditions that drive it.

Recovery encourages, even challenges us, to dig deep, explore causation, and replace our addictive tendencies with more useful and productive behaviors. It's more about the swapping than the stopping.

What if Shneidman's "psychache" could be turned around? What if instead of pain, we could see gratitude, instead of sadness, we could see contentment, instead of death, we could see life and opportunity?

These are the gifts of recovery. There are many of us to welcome you! In helping you, we continue to save ourselves. So don't be shy. Come in, we've been waiting for you!

If you are here, reading this, then there's a good chance you or someone close to you is in distress. You may feel that some of this book is irreverent and can't possibly meet you at the level of your pain. I hope it can.

This is tough stuff, no way around it, but as the old saying goes, "Pain is inevitable, suffering is optional."

ADDICTION IS A FAMILY DISEASE

Recovery is a way to mitigate suffering, and it's a lot more fun if laughter is part of the process. Recovery is not a dour enterprise.

Some people say it's more like a rollercoaster!

Will you strap in for the ride?

Cell Phone Thanksgiving

CHAPTER 3

The Addict: Delusion, Denial, Despair, & Dishonesty

Cunning, Baffling, Powerful

Love me at your peril. My mind seeks drugs, alcohol, and/or detrimental behaviors without my permission. My addictions are cunning, baffling, and powerful; they are rapacious predators that shred me and those close by. I often obsessively pursue them to feel better, no matter how horrible they make me feel.

I possess a great forgetter that allows me to deny the damage done until it's done again and again and again. And even then, I may stay in denial. Denial ensures that I will almost always sabotage my best intentions.

I will not give up my momentary dopamine rush, no matter what. I can't bear the truth of myself. So instead, I munch a bag of cookies and a half gallon of ice cream, or tell you what to do, or buy more stuff for my hoarder-packed house, or drink a six-pack, or smoke a joint, or try to run your life.

Or worse, I do something really dangerous and self-harming like cutting myself, or shooting heroin, or dropping some pills, or drinking to black out with no idea how I got home.

Some I might do only once. Some are gateways to my next addiction. A few I might not come back from. The one I'm doing now won't be enough forever. I will always need more.

Addiction is a gangster disease. We always pay eventually, one way or another.

What's it costing you?

I fail to live up to my standards, faster than I can lower them.

The algorithm of addiction is a confusing calculation. Addictions can be helpful in the moment but poisonous over time. Addicts may run out of money, friends, family, home, and sanity, but they never run out of ways to delude themselves.

That's because our addictive behaviors can feel so right!

As a "medicine," some of the things we take and do can quell our demons momentarily, helping us relax and manage our discomforts. They are the Band-Aids covering long suffered wounds and vulnerabilities deep below the surface.

They are soothing and effective in the short term, but if not moderated, they will manifest repeatedly, time after time, even when we are sick of them. They take over. Then all bets are off. Denial sets in and hides the truth as we are dragged into a life of despair. Some of us eventually see where we are. Many never do.

I'm going shopping; at least the salesman flirts with me.
The hair of the dog always soothes my hangover.
I like a joint to relax.
I love comfort food when I'm upset.
I need to work late; I don't want to go home.
Sure, I get mad, but I'm right!
I'll feel better when you change.
Just a couple more, what the hell.
I don't spend that much time gaming.
I may act stupid sometimes, but I like the attention.

Who's fooling who?

"They are the Band-Aids covering long suffered wounds and vulnerabilities deep below the surface."

You can always tell an addict, but you can't tell 'em much.

When in our disease, we addicts live on Planet Denial, and that planet is in a completely different solar system.

We can't logically explain addiction to anyone because addiction is not logical—especially when we're in the midst of it—either as the addict or as a family member close by.

Have you ever tried to talk to an addict?

When they are drunk or high or exhibiting compulsive behaviors, it's probably best not even to try. Even when sober, addicts employ a full arsenal of evasive deflections. The addict mind is relentless and undeterred.

> *I'm fine.*
> *I just need something to take the edge off.*
> *I'm too smart to get hooked.*
> *I don't have to, I just like to.*
> *I can stop whenever I want.*
> *I've got it under control.*
> *Good job, fine house, nice car ... what's the problem?*
> *Everybody deserves to enjoy life.*
> *I have more important things to deal with.*
> *It's not a problem, really.*
> *The kids are fine, just ask them.*
> *It's all good.*

What's really going on?

You can always tell an addict but you can't tell 'em much.

I can't hear you; my addiction is too loud.
"Yak-Yak-Yak-Yak-Yak-Yak...........Yakkety Yak!"

We addicts and our loved ones have a hard time listening and a harder time hearing.

I don't want to hear their advice, recriminations, assumptions, resentments, or self-pity. I have heard it all before, time after time after time. I feel contempt for every suggestion and meet nagging with anger or withdrawal.

Likewise, my loved ones, who can't stop trying to fix me, are tired of hearing the incessant excuses, lies, apologies, manipulations, angry outbursts, and selfishness I heap on them.

We end up locked in the same old tangle in every interaction— all immersed in a black hole of sadness, disappointment, guilt, shame, and regret.

These repetitive encounters, without resolution, are not fun or productive. I've experienced them from both sides. Most were pointless and only pushed us further apart.

Here's a quote often attributed to Herbert Spencer: "There is a principle which is a bar against all information, which is proof against all arguments, and which cannot fail to keep a man in everlasting ignorance—that principle is contempt prior to investigation."

THE ADDICT

The addict says:

Stop bugging me.
I don't want to hear it.
Worry about your own stuff.
You are the one who's making it all worse.
You're overreacting.
Recovery is bullshit—it's a religious cult.
They are all addicts and I'm not.
I can handle it myself.
Rehab is a waste of time and money.
It's all just psychobabble.
Don't talk to me about God!
That program is for losers.

The loved one says:

You must stop.
You're ruining your life.
Why won't you listen?
I can't imagine losing you.
You mean everything to me.
You're going to get hurt.
We must get you help.
I will find the right rehab.
I know someone you can talk to.

What is the power of listening without judgment?

"The worst of our behaviors will always sabotage the best of our dreams."
— Craig D. Lounsbrough

After my mother divorced my father, we lived with her most of the time. Once when she went on vacation, a young couple from the graduate school stayed with us to babysit.

One evening, he came home, and she ran from the kitchen to the front door to greet him in an embrace. It was a kind of embrace I had never seen before, free and warm and deeply loving.

I told her earlier in the day that my favorite truck had broken. She told him. They looked at me, still in each other's arms.

I showed him the toy. He asked me to get a pair of pliers and a screwdriver, and we sat down on the sofa next to each other and spread the project out on old newspaper on the coffee table.

He was a very kind man and was there in that moment for me—one hundred percent *there for me.*

I couldn't quite reach the tools, so I slipped off the couch onto my knees in front of the table. We took the toy apart.

He showed me how. Then he showed me what was wrong and how to fix it. And I did. Then he showed me how to put it back together. In the process, I got some grease on my finger and wiped it on his pant leg.

He looked down at what I had done, looked back at me, got up, and walked away. I have no memories of the couple after that.

I don't know why I rubbed the grease on his pants. It wasn't premeditated. I just did it. Maybe I was trying to be funny. Maybe I hurt him because he was the father I wanted but couldn't have.

Maybe I pushed him away because I couldn't tolerate such attention. Maybe I did it because he loved his wife, and I couldn't believe that was possible. I had never witnessed it before. I thought fighting and divorce were the norm. Maybe it happened because I was eight and didn't know better.

In the years since, often unconsciously, I've sabotaged other personal and professional relationships without fully knowing why.

Maybe I don't deserve them. Maybe self-sabotage is a symptom of my disease.

I am coming from nowhere fast and going nowhere faster. I can't resist. My brain and body are programmed.

I have no spirit left, except for the desire to escape it. It has been cleaved from me. I hate myself so much it's impossible to care about myself, or you, or anybody else.

The wounds have been buried so deep for so long that they scare me to death. I'll just hide under a rock.

I obsess over my addiction so much, it's hard to get other stuff done. I'm always sabotaging myself. I can't help it.

How do you sabotage yourself?

A Story

A friend told me a story about her son. He was speeding on the 405 freeway and got pulled over by the Highway Patrol. The officer exited his vehicle and walked to the driver's open window.

"Sir, do you know how fast you were going just now?"

"Oh wow, no, no, I, I'm not sure."

"Sir, could you turn down your radio?"

"Sure."

"Thank you," the officer says. "Actually, I clocked you at 110 miles an hour."

"What? Really? I didn't think this old buggy could go that fast."

"Evidently, it can." He shows the addict the radar gun.

"Yikes. Are you sure that's me?'

"Have you been drinking today, sir?"

"Oh no, officer. Absolutely not!"

"Are you aware that driving at 110 miles per hour could take innocent lives—including your own?"

"It's all good? Every one's ok, right?"

"Sir, please step out of the car."

This cop is getting on my nerves.
Come on, man, it's no big deal.
I drive better stoned anyway.
He's just busting my chops.
Such a pain!
I'm not hurting anybody.
I'm late for a party.
I can't believe he's patting me down.

What do you hear?

SOS: Stuck on Stupid

I once noticed an old woman sitting on her front porch with tubes in her nose and an oxygen bottle by her side, smoking a cigarette. I was fascinated.

She was withered and gaunt, with deep lines etched in her gray skin. She looked decrepit, but her motions were determined and efficient as she stubbed out her butt, grabbed the pack and lighter from her lap, and fired up another one.

Wary of oxygen and open flame I stepped back, thinking, "Here's someone dying of emphysema, and she's still smoking! Hello?!"

Then I recalled my own smoking history. Was I any smarter?

No!

I was stuck on stupid too. I wasn't thinking at all when I started smoking. I smoked for almost twenty years. My apartment stank, my car stank, my clothes stank, I stank. Finally, my fiancé said, "It's me or the cigarettes!" I quit.

It's so easy to slip into some of these behaviors and so hard to escape them.

Those of us who are addicted are often wrong but rarely in doubt. Our behavior is repetitive. Even if we know we should quit, we invariably cycle back into the behavioral loop.

We can't seem to help ourselves. Willpower doesn't last long; it's outmatched by addiction. We feel powerless, and left to our own devices, we are.

I'm not stupid, but smoking was stupid. Addiction is a disease of deceptive perceptions cloaked in denial.

I ran miles every day to stay in shape and still smoked. I was prone to chest colds and sinus infections. I kept smoking.

Did I correlate the two? Rarely. And even when I did, I would only stop briefly. We addicts are naturally non-compliant, and often oppositional, fearing the light of truth and honesty.

Heck, we lie to ourselves for so long that it's hard to tell the truth.

Where are you stuck?

Isolation protects me from you, but not from myself.

Addictions foster secrets. These secrets separate us from others in many ways: physically, emotionally, and spiritually. We withdraw into ourselves to hide our unmentionable tendencies. We are ashamed of them. They are corrosive.

We are social animals, but when wounded and sick our first instinct may be to withdraw. We feel like locking the door, lowering the blinds, or running away until we get better.

But separation from you won't protect me from myself. My mind, which is already diseased, is not thinking straight— often it's abusive, angry, irritable, and discontent.

I have to hide what's going on.
I'll lie about most of it.
If I tell you what's really going on, you'll nag me to death.
I don't want to quit.
If I admit my failings, you'll abandon me.
It's safer to keep to myself.
If you see what I'm really like, you'll despise me.
I'll just hole up for a while and figure this out on my own.

Addicts treat loneliness with further isolation. It's like treating lung cancer with cigarettes.

Once we see the truth of our situation and are willing to make substantive changes, we need others to support and guide us.

We need friends and loved ones; perhaps counselors, therapists, in-patient care, out-patient care, meetings, and other tools. That's why recovery programs are *WE* programs, not *I* programs.

Who can you confide in?

"...I look at myself in the mirror...and think to myself that I am a liar."

CHAPTER 4

The Family

"Addiction is a family disease."

The Family Disease

If I could go back to the beginning of my addiction, knowing what I know now, I would warn you:

> *I am sick, and my disease will make you sick too.*
> *It will make your life miserable.*
> *I will use your love to manipulate and control you.*
> *I will steal from you, lie to you, and trick you into doing things for me that I should be doing for myself.*
> *My addiction will turn you into an addict too—addicted to caring for me, fixing me, changing me, and saving me.*
> *You won't know it's happening until it's too late.*
> *You can't save me, but you can save yourself.*
> *So ... don't you dare love me! Love yourself instead.*

It helps to know that our problem is well understood. Here's a passage from *Paths to Recovery*, the handbook of Al-Anon, the international support group for families and friends of those affected by the disease of alcoholism.

> "[T]he alcoholism of one member affects the whole family, and all become sick. Why does this happen? Unlike diabetes, addiction not only exists inside the body of the addict but is a disease of relationship as well. Many of the symptoms of alcoholism are in the behavior of the alcoholic—and also appear in the loved one. The people who are involved with the alcoholic react to this behavior. They try to control it, make up for it, or hide it. They often blame themselves for it and are hurt by it. Eventually, they become emotionally disturbed themselves."

What's familiar for you?

Trapped and Clueless

For those of us who love an addict, the heartbreak can be relentless and unbearable. At first, we can be clueless. Then we might start seeing signs but choose to ignore them. We give our addict the benefit of the doubt, telling ourselves:

> *Kids will be kids. She'll outgrow it.*
> *It's best not to overreact.*
> *My husband's too successful to have a drug problem.*
> *Well, she's got to eat.*
> *Oh, he only parties on the weekends.*
> *I thought she stopped going to the casino.*

Then things might get so bad our selective awareness or denial can no longer shield us from what's so obvious to others. We are finally forced to admit that someone we love has a real problem. It can be so scary that we jump in to fix it, and we keep trying to fix it—relentlessly

This compulsion to fix and save can be as powerful as any drug. We can't stop telling them what to do, how to straighten up, how to get better. And it's this very struggle that can defeat us too.

Love dictates that we accomplish the impossible.

> *Of course, I will help if my addict needs help!*
> *I'll do whatever it takes, even sacrifice myself.*
> *How could I do otherwise?*

We become trapped in this family disease of hidden consequences. It can come as a shock. It did for me.

What's happening?

Love me at your peril.

The road to hell is paved with good intentions.

I am your relative, your friend, or your employer trying to help. I have an addiction too.
  My addiction is to you.
  I want to save you, fix you, make you over again.
  I want to support you, heal you, pay your bills, keep you out of trouble, keep you employed.
  I will do anything to manage you and your disease, to make things look good and to cover for you.
  You are my responsibility, my liability, my curse, and my salvation.

I understand these feelings. I know how impossible it is to fix someone you care about. I tried with my father, my brother, and my son.

The more I tried to change things for the better, the crazier life became for all of us.

In dealing with our son, our marriage was stressed and broken. Our other kids became resentful as we focused on his problems. We became more and more obsessed as we saw things crumbling around us.

We were overwhelmed, scooped out, but still tried to manage everything to keep up appearances.

Our son could be aggressive, even violent, making our home unsafe.

We started doubting our choices, doubting ourselves, doubting each other, feeling depressed, sad, lonely, guilty, ashamed, and terrified that either our son might die, or we might go crazy.

The truth is brutal. If you ain't a lion tamer, stay out of the cage.

We didn't cause his addiction, we couldn't control it, and we couldn't cure it. That slogan is what Al-Anon calls the Three Cs, and it helped me in early recovery.

There is a suggested fourth "C"—Stop contributing to it. And even a fifth—Stop competing with it.

In recovery, we were encouraged to focus on our own health instead of abandoning ourselves in service to our son's disease.

We learned to take responsibility for ourselves, put on our own life preservers first. Set an example. Perhaps something would rub off—perhaps.

It wasn't disloyal. It's what we had to do. All else was fantasy and magical thinking.

No one ever got sober because of the demands and expectations of others—only through awareness of oneself.

How is fixing things making things worse?

"If you ain't a lion tamer, stay out of the cage."

If you try to compete with addiction, you've already lost.

Addiction is offensive, but those of us closest to it live on the defensive. We try to react fast enough, appropriately enough, and effectively enough, but we can't.

That's because we are always behind the action. Life with an addict is always in motion, always spinning, even shapeshifting. Most of the time we don't know the score. We can't even tell what side we're on.

Addiction is a free-for-all—no rules and time limit. Chaos ensues. Attrition follows. Victories are hollow and temporary. People die.

How can we compete? Professionals working in addiction recovery understand that the odds are always stacked against them and their patients.

They were stacked against me too.

My eldest lived with me during the height of his illness. His third treatment center couldn't tolerate his violent behavior. They told me to come and get him or they would call the police.

I took him in, hoping I could help him, knowing deep down that I couldn't. I loved him. I couldn't let him go to jail. Jail was his greatest fear.

He lived with me for nine months. On day three, I was already in urgent care, having what I thought was a heart attack. It turned out to be a panic attack. I was out of my depth.

His paranoia, insomnia, neediness, violent and irrational behavior all contributed to my mental decline over those nine months.

I was incapable of helping him, and trying to do so made me sick too.

Something so caring and seemingly benign, my desire to help, eventually put me in the hospital, then a psych ward.

It was all too much—everything felt impossible. I should have done nothing.

That's right. In many cases the solution is nothing.

I can detest his disease and also love him.

I will always love him.

Anything beyond that is too painful and usually futile.

What are you tolerating?

The Red Tattoo

They might have bought you a ticket for the crazy train, but you don't have to board.

I remember when my son got his first tattoo—all over his left arm: four red concentric circles interrupted every inch by a small square. At the time, he was heavy into boxing, but he would never share the significance of the design. It meant something special to him, but I couldn't see it. Though outwardly accepting, I was screaming inside:

How could you do that to my arm?
You're my son, so your arm is mine too.
This tattoo is permanent and irreversible.
We can never get rid of it.
You have disfigured us.

I clearly had a proprietary interest in the state of his arm.

It took a few days for me to wake up and realize that my possessiveness was wacko. He loved his tat. I could see that, I didn't understand it. So what?

Eventually, I came to see that his arm and his tattoo had nothing to do with me. It was his arm, his tattoo, his life, his choice. It helped define his independence. It was his act of self-determination.

My addiction was my dependence on him (and his arm). Part of my value was determined by this attachment.

I had to let go. I stopped talking and started listening. In time, I grew to love his tattoo just as I loved him.

What would happen if you let go?

Enabling Is Disabling

"I'm not controlling, I just know what's best for you," says the rescuing parent, lover, friend, spouse, or employer.

But, if I'm honest with myself, I must confess that much of this is about me, not you. My insecurities, my co-dependence, my need for others' validation, including yours. I feel compelled to rescue you because I have no idea how to rescue myself. I don't even believe I need rescuing.

I will lie for you.
I will always step in.
I will make things right.
I will hire lawyers, doctors, and counselors.
I will minimize your consequences.
I will throw money at your problems.
I will do for you what you should be doing for yourself.

I can't possibly admit that my own behavior, far from helping, is only making things worse. When I enable you, I distort your perception of reality. I make you dependent on me. The message I send is "You're not capable enough, strong enough, or intelligent enough to survive, so *I'm* going to pick up the pieces and put you back together again." I may even unknowingly support your bad habits.

An even subtler form of enabling is to do it by proxy. I might decide to hold the line but stay silent when my partner, grandparent, sibling, relative, or employer enables instead. If there is no clear consensus on boundaries by all the loved ones, the would-be helpers work at cross-purposes.

How could you be disabling someone you love?

When you hold too tight, you can strangle.

There's a scene in the John Steinbeck novella *Of Mice and Men* that illustrates how affection can be fatal.

Lennie, a simple-minded ranch hand who doesn't know his own strength, is attracted to Curley's wife, a flirty tart with soft hair. She likes it when Lennie strokes her hair but gets scared and struggles when she feels his strength. Sensing trouble, he covers her mouth to keep her from crying out. The more she struggles, the harder he squeezes. He panics, squeezes too hard, and breaks her neck.

As we try to keep our addicts close and safe, we can hold on too tightly. We suffocate them and undermine any desire they might have to take responsibility for their own lives.

We become enmeshed because we make assumptions about the severity of their need, often unconsciously serving our own.

What we don't realize is that by bringing them close, we are choosing to bring their disease close. We bring it into our personal space, and like a virus, it infects us too, though perhaps in different ways. We believe that the strength of our love will defeat their addiction. In most cases, the strength of our addiction to them defeats us.

The bottom line: *loosen your grip*. Don't be a Lennie.

Create space so you can see the whole picture more objectively, less emotionally. Learn the facts about addiction and understand your part in the dance. Or better yet, learn the facts and sit out the dance—that way, no one will step on your toes.

What would it mean to loosen your grip?

CHAPTER 5

Living With Myself

How Can I

Living with the decision to turn away from an addict can feel devastating. The guilt can be even worse if the addict is a child, parent, or sibling.

How can I live with myself when I finally say "Enough"?
How can I live with myself the day I turn away from my child, my spouse, or my friend?
How can I forgive myself when I call the police?
How can I live with myself the day he goes to jail, and I won't bail him out?
How can I live with myself the day she is homeless, and I won't let her back in my house?

"I trusted you!" I can still hear the blame, the accusations. "You did this to me, it's all your fault. I will never forgive you!"

How can I survive his violent outbursts?
How can I endure her paranoia, fear, and rage?
How can I live with the constant blame and recrimination?
What did I do to deserve this?
Was this really my fault?
Was I such a bad parent?
Didn't I do my best?

We may doubt ourselves when we detach, but somewhere deep inside there's relief as well, relief in surrender, relief from trying to dictate another's life, relief from the constant grief of witnessing our addict self-destruct—relief in accepting powerlessness.

How can you?

You can't be rational with an addict because addiction isn't rational.

I imagine that the titanic ship *Addiction* is sinking in rough seas, taking all the passengers to their watery graves. I am frantically rowing the lifeboat to my daughter, who is swimming to me, struggling, freezing, and gasping for air.

I reach her, pull her into the lifeboat *Recovery*, and wrap her in a warm blanket. She is shivering, her lips blue, but she is safe, thank God.

We huddle for warmth with our fellow passengers, watching the ship go down. Everyone knows it's a miracle that they are alive when so many others have perished.

Suddenly, my daughter throws off her blanket and shouts, "That wasn't so bad, I'm going back in!" And she does, diving over the gunnel into the roiling blackness.

She takes a few strokes, then slips under and disappears. Terror strikes me and takes over!

I have to go after her!
She is my daughter. My only daughter!
It's my duty!

I jump. I jump in this story, just as I jumped in real life.

I jumped in to save her every time she relapsed.

Luckily someone always grabbed me before I sank and pulled me back into the boat. But I kept diving in again and again and she kept slipping through my fingers. I almost drowned.

I was lost but finally saved with the help of others and the miracle of recovery. Now I stay in the boat.

I have learned my lesson. I can't save someone who doesn't want to be saved.

How can you stay in the lifeboat?

"It's hard to save someone who doesn't want to be saved."

Caring For, Not Taking Care Of

I don't *take care of* my addict anymore, but I still *care for* her deeply.

What's obvious now is that I was never the way; I was generally *in* the way. My attachment addiction had no bounds. I would do almost anything to relieve her pain, even at the cost of creating my own.

I did not amputate her from my life. Her addiction amputated me. I had to let her go. In the end, I learned to detach with love, or even better, detach *to* love.

When she left, she took her love from me, a love I could never imagine losing. It felt like all the love in my world was gone. I was left with nothing.

Or so I thought. In fact, she did not carry my love for her in her suitcase when she walked out the door. I still had it, no matter what. I could still nurture it and let it nurture me.

True, there was nothing I could do if she chose to withdraw her love from me, but it was never mine to begin with. I only thought it was.

I learned to cherish this new way of caring for her—separate from her disease.

My job now is to get well, recover my lost self, and get ready if she ever chooses to re-enter my life.

I need to be a different person if she comes back. I need to relinquish any sense of control. I need to put judgment aside and accept her as she is.

Maybe we can be different then, grown in understanding and acceptance. Maybe I won't make the same mistakes. Maybe, just maybe, we can get to know each other in new ways.

I'll always care for her and love her, but I no longer take care of her. It's enough to take care of myself.

Who do you care for, but can no longer take care of?

If Only

You have stepped aside. You feel momentary relief. You have a new sense of freedom, tentative though it may be. You can't believe that today you don't have to go to war with their addiction. But oddly, you don't know what to do with yourself.

Now the second-guessing begins—the bargaining—the inner debate. Shame and guilt keep coming up. Your mind won't let you rest.

You start wondering if you made a mistake.

If only I hadn't been so angry.
If only I had listened more.
If only my father hadn't been a drunk too.
If only I had spotted the problem sooner.
If only I had sent him to a different doctor.
If only I had warned her about fentanyl.
If only I hadn't sent him to that wilderness camp.
If only I could have gotten through to her.
 If only my marriage was stronger.
If only I were better. If only! If only! If only!

I have fanaticized a million options, a million ways to do better, a million ways to still make it all right. I had let go, but my heart was still struggling with the separation, so my mind kept churning solutions.

But no matter how hard I tried, I couldn't change the past or dictate the future. There's nothing disloyal about choosing our own survival.

How does your guilt help you get better?

The Leftovers

I loved my younger brother and resented him too. He treated his mental illness by self-medicating. Life was a constant struggle for him and for our whole family.

Whenever my mother and I talked, her first question was, "How's your brother?" I was her middleman, appeasing her by helping him. I tried to keep him out of trouble, support him, and help him turn his life around.

After a while, I started resenting being in the middle. When it came to her attention and affection, I felt like a leftover.

I started getting upset and resentful. When we talked, I would think,

Hold on a second, why aren't you asking about me?
Why is it always about him?
What am I, chopped liver?

Eventually, I grew to understand that she viewed me as her ally in saving him. To some degree, I mattered most as an intermediary. After all, I was the middle child, he my younger brother.

I felt a duty to her and guilt for having success when he had little. She felt guilty about his sad life and became so obsessed with it that my sister and I became secondary.

I don't blame my mother. It's all she knew. She felt it her sacred duty to try to save her youngest child. She failed; he died before her. I too have wanted to save my own children. I repeated her mistakes.

While trying to manage our older son's mental health and addiction issues, we were not able to give our younger son the attention he deserved.

He was an easy baby, able to self-soothe and sleep. As a toddler, he seemed self-sufficient, calm, and centered. We were overwhelmed, and he suffered for it.

It's hard for the leftovers to feel fully loved, and the results can be far-reaching. Like addiction, they can span generations.

Who's not fully recognized in your family?

"I didn't feel safe as the family exploded."

If I'm not the addict, why the hell do I need recovery?

This makes no sense.
You're the addict, but I need recovery?
You're the one who needs help, not me.
This whole idea really makes me furious!
This isn't my fault!

Let's say you go to a party, and you learn the next day that your hostess was sick without knowing it and passed on a contagious virus. Two days later, you test positive and start to experience symptoms. Ugh!

Chances are you'll spend the next several days checking your temperature, staying in bed, and drinking liquids. Maybe you'll see the doctor and take some meds.

Whatever you feel about your hostess, it's a good bet that won't stop you from doing whatever it takes to get better. Even if you're mad at her, will you refuse to seek treatment?

Similarly, would you refuse treatment because you were mad at someone who exposed you to the disease of addiction?

If you had parents who drank too much, a friend who was a control freak, a spouse with a drug problem, an anorexic child, a relative with a gambling habit—then you have been exposed to the disease.

Whether you are aware of it or not, you may already be experiencing some of the effects of the disease: anxiety, depression, guilt, shame, anger, frustration, overwhelm, sleeplessness.

You deserve to get better too, don't you?

How are you doing?

The Dos and Don'ts

The Al-Anon Family Groups have provided us who love an alcoholic with a list of guidelines for acting and reacting in the face of *our* struggles with *their* disease. This list also works well with navigating other addictions. When I started recovery in the Al-Anon program, I got straight As in the ***don'ts*** and had real trouble doing the ***dos.***

I'm happy to say that over the years, this has shifted a lot. Now I subscribe whole-heartedly to the ***dos*** and am aware of the ***don'ts*** mostly when I slip on them. Let's read them in reverse order. to save the best for last.

The don'ts:
Don't be self-righteous.
Don't try to dominate, nag, scold, or complain.
Don't lose your temper.
Don't try to push anyone but yourself.
Don't keep bringing up the past.
Don't keep checking up on your alcoholic.
Don't wallow in self-pity.
Don't make threats you don't intend to carry out.
Don't be over-protective.
Don't be a doormat.

The dos:
Do forgive.
Do be honest with yourself.
Do be humble.
Do take it easy, tension is harmful.
Do play. Have fun—find recreation and hobbies.
Do keep on trying whenever you fail.

Do learn all the facts about alcoholism.
Do attend Al-Anon meetings regularly.

*How do these resonate in your relationship
with your addict?*

CHAPTER 6

The Awakening

"Desperation is the raw material of drastic change."
— William Burroughs

We don't come into recovery because our lives are great. We come in when our desperation is greater than our resistance.

Many people now living happy lives without substances or other bad habits were unable to turn their lives around until things got so bad they simply couldn't stand it anymore. They had hit bottom.

For some, the truth of their predicament comes in a flash. For others, it's only a glimmer, but that glimmer can be enough. That's why many sober addicts say their deepest desperation was their greatest gift.

It's often triggered by circumstance: a traffic stop, a doctor's word, a judge's verdict, a self-inflicted wound, the mistrust in a lover's eyes.

Some people simply look in a mirror and see themselves for who they really are—powerless over addiction, substances, other people, or destructive behaviors. It's often painful.

I can't take this anymore.
I'm sick. I need help!
It really is killing me, just like they said.
I love them so, and I'm hurting them.
It's all a house of cards!
I could have killed my kids driving drunk!
I can't do this for the rest of my life.
Please God, no more!

ADDICTION IS A FAMILY DISEASE

The instant we acknowledge our problem we can begin—if we are willing. At this moment we have a choice.

We can ask for help and begin to recover, or we can deny the truth and continue the downward spiral—trapped, until the next time we are jolted back to reality.

What's your choice?

My ego is not my amigo.

The first time I quit drinking, I did it cold turkey. We had young children. It was better for all concerned if I didn't drink, especially during those tough kid-rearing hours in the evening.

So, I quit. My wife offered the suggestion, to put it mildly, and I listened to her. I wish I had sought active recovery then.

Though I stopped drinking, my problems persisted. I was still stuck with my obsessive thinking, my fears, my resentments, and my faults. They were sharper than ever without the soothing effects of alcohol.

I discovered that quitting an addiction cold turkey and isolating is a very lonely business.

I needed help. But I didn't want to admit it. I had lots of reasons, and they all seemed valid.

I don't have time.
I'm not nearly as bad as those people.
I've always managed on my own.
Recovery is all sanctimonious nonsense.
What's with the God thing anyway?
The rehab I want doesn't have a place for me.
Oh please! Don't you know who I am?

What really stopped me was pride. Ego and denial overwhelmed my common sense.

As time passed, the initial euphoria and clarity I experienced when I first stopped drinking morphed into a fuzzy dim trudge.

Even though my body was free of alcohol, my addictive thinking persisted. In the long run, I couldn't manage it on my own. Years later, alcohol caught up with me again.

How are your reasons holding you back?

My Bottom

I hit my bottom on Christmas 2014. The family was together at home for the first time since my wife and I had separated. There was some tension, but it was a nice holiday.

At the end of the day, my youngest son and I went back to my apartment. At sixteen, he had been in recovery for three years. I hadn't had a drink in fifteen years, so he had never seen me drunk.

Later that evening, I decided I needed some time on my own. I told him I was going to church. At least, that's what he told me years later. I don't remember.

Instead of going to the little church down the street for the late Christmas service, I stopped in at a bar. Instead of the club soda with lime I usually drank, I ordered a gin and tonic. Then another.

I had no defense against that first drink. And no defense against what followed.

I do remember talking to a few people, but it's hazy. I woke up at four in the morning in a puddle of drool, face plastered to the sidewalk near my car. What had happened during the hours I was unconscious? Did I hurt anyone? Was I robbed? Where were my glasses?

A sweet little man in a Santa hat picked me up, poured me into my car and said, "Don't drive! Sleep it off."

I drove home, squinting through the windshield. I had lost my glasses. I staggered up to my apartment, expecting my son to be asleep. He wasn't. The disappointment, sadness, and hurt in his eyes crushed me.

"I gotta go," he said. "I don't feel safe." And he did. We didn't speak much for the next five years.

My bottom was the moment I saw the look of distrust, sadness, and pain in his eyes. Sober himself, he knew he had to turn away from me to protect himself. I was proud of him for that.

But it broke my heart. I couldn't manage my thoughts, my life, or my behavior.

I had lost control.
I couldn't stand myself anymore.
I was ready to change.
I wanted my sobriety back.
I joined a recovery program.
I started listening.
I stopped judging
I stopped defending.

I realized I was living the wrong life. Pain convinced me that I had no power over my drinking addiction. Later I learned, much to my dismay, that I had no power over others' addictions either.

Have you reached your bottom?

"He told me later that I told him I was going to church."

You can't save face and your ass at the same time

When we get out of control, we often hurt others and have plenty to be ashamed of. I had secrets I was going to take to my grave, but my friends in recovery told me if I didn't come clean about them, I'd probably drink again.

Still, I resisted.

> *No, no, no, no, no, I've been holding onto that one for years!*
> *I don't even want to think about it, let alone tell you.*
> *There are good reasons people don't talk about private things.*
> *Better to forget it—bury it deep.*

If this was the direction treatment was taking, count me out.

When I talked about my fears with a trusted recovery friend, he said, "You're only as sick as your secrets."

Sometimes we need to look bad before we can look good. Recovery involves admitting our faults to ourselves, and if we are serious about changing, it means admitting them to others and repairing what damage we can.

We've been doing things our way for so long that changing means swallowing a lot of pride. Examining hard truths about ourselves can be daunting.

We may feel vulnerable, at risk. That's one of the many reasons so few people are able to recover on their own. We have to start being honest about ourselves, with ourselves, and with others.

Getting better doesn't always feel better, especially at first. It takes courage to face the truth, but the truth really does set us free.

What's the secret you want to release?

Ice Cream and Cookies

Most people can get physically sober after a few days or weeks of detox. That's how it worked for me. The hard part is staying clean day after day.

That's how we do it—day after day, one day at a time— because addiction is a physical and mental disease. Our bodies are speedy healers. Our minds, not so much.

"Why do you keep going to those meetings?" friends ask me. "You haven't had a drink in years."

I answer, "Because altering my thinking takes time. It's something I have to work on a little bit every day, and I'll probably never complete the job."

Old-timers in A.A. call it "stinkin' thinkin'," and it never stops.

As I'm writing this, I begin ruminating about oatmeal raisin cookies. Meg's restaurant around the corner makes the best ones ever—crisp and chewy at the same time.

I can already taste the first bite, that burst of flavor.
I'll eat a couple on the walk back home.
Just two.
When did this chair get so uncomfortable?
Two is good.
There are ten in the bag, but I'll only have two.
I'll save the rest for later.

I remind myself what the doc said about my sugar intake and decide I need exercise, not cookies. I head for the cross trainer. It's a good workout. Fifteen minutes, twenty …

I'll do forty-five minutes.
If I do forty-five good, hard minutes, then I can go for cookies.
Working that sugar out in advance.
I'll deserve a reward. No guilt.

The phone rings. It's a business partner, and I stay busy for the next several hours.

I wish I had something to nibble with this coffee.
I wish he wasn't so long-winded.
This doesn't have to be so complicated.
It's getting late.
Awww noooo, Meg's is closed!

Good! I made it through the day without succumbing. I deserve a little pat on the back, I reckon. Then hours later, I end up at the little market around the corner buying some crummy, overpriced cookies. And two pints of ice cream.

Oh, and some dark chocolate with sea salt.
I missed out on Meg's cookies.
I'll make up in quantity what I lost in quality.
More is better.

I pig out on stuff I didn't really want and wake up the next morning feeling guilty with a nasty sugar hangover. Almost like old times. Sure, ice cream and cookies aren't gin and tonic. They didn't make me do anything stupid, hurtful, or criminal.

It's been nine years since I had a drink, but addiction thinking is alive and well in my noggin. I can't afford to ignore it.

Where is your attention directed??

"I'm not responsible for my first thought, but I am responsible for those that follow."

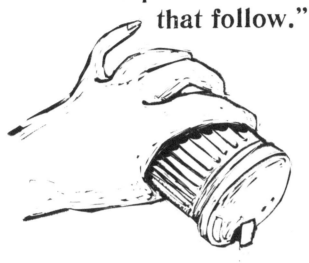

Don't leave before the miracle.

An acquaintance told me about her son. He was arrested and would have to detox in jail.

He'd been on the street for three years, and all he cared about was heroin and money to get more heroin. She decided not to bail him out this time. She had done it so many times before. She knew she was addicted to helping and fixing him. She was consumed by his need. But her efforts were not helping. She decided to stop.

Weeks later, after he had detoxed, she went to see him in jail. He was contrite and humbled, and he looked her in the eye and thanked her. "For what?" she said. He said, "For not bailing me out, for giving me a chance to get clean, a chance to have a life."

She was touched but had fallen for his lies many times and wondered if he was being honest. It turned out he was.

When I talked to her later, she was thrilled. Something had changed. There was a new light in his eyes; he was sober for the first time in years, wanted recovery, and was willing to live in a halfway house after jail. He had a chance.

It was a big deal for him and for her. She had been afraid he would die on the street.

These miracles happen in recovery every day. They fuel our hope and our commitment.

They're not always big miracles, either.

Like making a phone call when you need support, or brewing coffee at a meeting, or supporting someone in crisis, or reading recovery literature, or simply sitting and meditating in gratitude for another day free from the bondage of the disease.

It's easy to believe in miracles when you see them happening all around you.

What could be your miracle?

CHAPTER 7

The Toolbox

The Tools

Just as we endure our own personal form of addiction, we must each explore our own form of recovery. Few of us can do it without help.

Professionals and sober addicts often talk about having a *toolbox* packed with gadgets that assist in fixing broken behaviors and broken thinking.

They help us develop the capacity to do the work to unveil, process, and share the pain, distortion, and dysfunction of our current reality.

The tools may vary depending on the type of intervention, but some are generally applicable to all types of recovery.

It's important to remember that the most powerful gizmos on earth won't help if they're left hidden in the toolbox.

Take them out and learn how to use them.

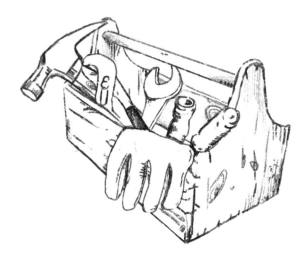

"We've acquired new tools. Now it's time to bear down and get to work."

Surrender

When I hit bottom and admitted defeat, I already posessed one of the most powerful tools in recovery but I didn't know it at the time.

Surrender: I didn't have a chance of winning my battle with addiction until I quit fighting.

We hear people say, "I gave up cigarettes" or "I gave up booze" or "I gave up tellimg my husband what to do." For me, it was more like, "I give up, stop punching me!"

For the first time, and I hope the last time, I was done, and I knew it.

No more, please!
I'm beat up from the feet up.
Tore up from the floor up
What am I fighting for?
There's no point in this.
If I surrender, perhaps new options will arise.

This was a new revelation, and I have no idea where it came from. I consider it a miracle.

So often my engagement with addiction felt like a thousand-round heavyweight bout. A test of strength and will, punch after punch after punch.

Stop the bleeding. Win a round. Patch a cut. Lose two rounds. On and on. Eventually, I learned to leave my gloves at the gym. As a sober friend told me,

ADDICTION IS A FAMILY DISEASE

**You don't have to attend every
argument you're invited to.**

I finally got it. I threw in the towel. I surrendered. I understood my powerlessness.

How can you stop fighting?

"You don't have to attend every argument you are invited to."

Commitment

Whenever I hear someone say addicts have no willpower, I have to laugh. Nobody has more willpower than an alcoholic or addict in pursuit of their objective.

Remember how relentless and resourceful you could be when it came to your own addiction? That means you've got the right stuff: commitment. Be as committed to recovery as you were to your addiction.

Commitment no matter what.

Many people have a hard time with the idea of going the rest of their lives without their habitual behaviors of using, controlling, escaping, and denying. That's why recovery has slogans like:

One step at a time.
Just for today.
Keep coming back.
Do the next indicated action.

At first, I couldn't commit to changing my life forever. That was just too much to swallow all at once. GULP!

But I could commit to making changes a day at a time or until tomorrow. When tomorrow came, I made another commitment to that day. Days turned to weeks, to months, to years, one day at a time.

The very act of starting in recovery can seem counterintuitive, contrary, foreign, and scary. It's a step into the unknown, it takes a certain fierceness of purpose.

Can you stop taking that substance today, can you stop fixing someone else today, can you stay away from the casino today, can you throw away the sweets today, can you pour out that bottle of gin today, can you stop that behavior today? Commitment is driven by courage.

What will you commit to today?

Fellowship

I went without a drink for fifteen years. It was lonely and tenuous—I ultimately failed. Where addiction is concerned, willpower has its limitations.

Unfortunately, I was taking advice from myself—not recommended.

Finally, desperate, depressed, and despondent, I gave up and joined a recovery program. I went to three or four twelve-step meetings and felt very much the outsider.

I had a lot of shame and guilt. I couldn't hear the message. I was too upset, self-conscious, and alone.

At my fifth meeting, a guy walked up and wrapped a welcome around me that was utterly irresistible. Smiling, with hand outstretched, he said, "Hey, my name's Jack. Come in, we've been waiting for you!"

Me?
How did he know I was coming?
Holy mackerel.
I'm a total mess.
But he's glad to see me!
They all are!

This welcome was the beginning of my journey. Jack would become my mentor. He taught me how to get started and what I could expect. He became my sponsor in recovery.

He said my disease was lurking out there, just waiting to catch me alone again. "Stay close," he said again and again.

Some of my new friends amazed me. Their stories were worse than mine! Lost homes, lost jobs, lost families, even destitute, living on the streets. But they were happy folks laughing at sad things. They had problems like everybody else, but they were handling them, they had perspective, and they were getting on with their lives.

When my own family wouldn't have me, this recovery family took me in. I saw how they handled tragedies of family deaths, divorces, alienation, and bankruptcy without going back to their addictions.

I started opening up, sharing my story. I wanted what they had, so I began to do what they did.

How long has it been since you've felt like you belonged?

HOW?

HOW is the Swiss Army Knife of recovery. You can do practically anything with it and not much without it. It's three tools in one: honesty, openness, and willingness.

We addicts are masters of denial and self-deception. Countless times, I failed to listen to the truth. I didn't want to face it. I was selfish, languishing in the comfort of my own delusions.

> *Oh, I can manage him.*
> *It wasn't my fault.*
> *They'll never find out.*
> *Nobody cares anyway.*
> *I never hurt anybody.*
> *Where are my breath mints?*

My friend, guide, and shepherd in recovery emphasized the importance of *HOW*. When I started working with him, I was sure I could be honest, open, and willing. Of course, I would follow his lead and take his suggestions.

It was harder than I thought.

I was surprised how much resistance remained locked inside. It took time for me to trust him and the process.

Then, one sunny day sitting in his back yard, all those fears, secrets, resentments, and harms that had been simmering for years burst out of me.

This kind of truth-telling is profound. It's disruptive in a good way, a bit scary, but a great relief. No more secrets.

That's one of the reasons many recovery programs protect their members' anonymity—to make it easier for us to be open and honest.

It's amazing how free we can feel when we have nothing to hide.

What's stopping you from being honest, open, and willing?

"...find a shepherd to guide you, commit to the journey and thrive in a whole new world..."

Humility and Faith

In the early stages of recovery, I felt emotionally overwhelmed. I still struggled with my impulses to control, to know the answers, to hide, and to pretend I was better than I felt.

I was a bundle of contradictions. I thought I knew it all, but what I thought I knew hadn't worked. The denial of my personal problems hadn't worked, my escape into alcohol hadn't worked, my attempt to run others' lives hadn't worked, my sense of entitlement, my marriage, my obsessive analyzing hadn't worked.

For most of my life I was too proud to admit that my life wasn't working.

Recovery was a leap of faith that was years in the making— the choosing of a different reality, a leap into the huge space of unknowing. It seemed daunting, but I had no choice. I did it anyway.

This leap of faith was terrifying but also exhilarating— calling forth faith that I would survive, that on bad days the sun would rise, that I would have a chance to get well, and that there were better days and new opportunities to come.

I set aside what I thought I knew about life, addiction, recovery, and just about everything else. I was humbled in the knowledge that I was on the wrong track and had much to learn.

If everything was okay, I wouldn't be at this critical crossroads. My thinking and my actions got me here. Maybe some humble pie was a good idea—right sizing my ego—chopping wood and carrying water like everyone else.

I had to be willing to admit I didn't have the answers, to trust in the process, to trust in the group, my sponsor, and my therapist.

I had to be willing to reach out even when the phone felt heavy—like a thousand pounds heavy. I had to have the faith and humility to turn my messy life over to something, almost anything, greater than myself.

How is self-reliance working for you?

Forgiveness/Relapse

Not everybody gets it right the first time or even the second. One of the beautiful things about recovery is we learn to forgive ourselves and others.

Forgiveness is not only beautiful; it's essential. If I'm going to live happily with my less-than-perfect family and friends, I need to be willing to forgive, sometimes daily. The same goes for less-than-perfect me—the hard part.

I need to accept my mistakes, failures, and errors in judgment to avoid the downward spiral of guilt and shame that can make escape back into addiction seem inviting.

If my new friends in recovery hadn't been so forgiving after my relapse, I might not be here today. They said things like,

Welcome home!
We're glad to see you.
One day at a time, that's all we have.
The best we will ever be is human.
It takes what it takes.
We don't shoot our wounded.

Relapse, though it may seem like abject failure, can be an important milestone. If it's miserable enough, and it usually is, it can make us more determined than ever not to return to the old life.

It can be a chance to step back, get a clearer view, and recommit.

Many who relapse don't come back. I was lucky. I knew it. I grabbed my second chance and I'm still clinging to it today.

What can you forgive?

"The beauty of recovery is we don't shoot our wounded."

Persistence

Just as addiction is a way of life, so is recovery.

As an alcoholic, I will always be addicted to alcohol, whether I'm drinking or not. As a co-dependant I will always be addicted to control, whether I'm controlling or not. These are chronic conditions and they require consistant treatment.

The refrain in recovery is "Keep coming back!"

Even if you don't want to, keep coming back.
Even if you slip, keep coming back.
Even if it hurts and you feel miserable, keep coming back.
Even if you hate it, keep coming back.
Even if you think it's stupid, keep coming back.

In the beginning, when my addiction and my recovery were fighting for supremacy, I asked my sponsor, "How long do I have to keep coming back." It was hard at first and not much fun.

He said, "There are only two times when you should keep coming back: when you want to, and when you don't want to."

He also had another equally annoying saying, "Keep coming back until you want to come back."

Sometimes the beginning can be challenging and confusing. Many people stick with their program for weeks and months and even years only to relapse, go out, or slip. The best response is automatic: *COME BACK!*

The principals and tools of recovery are straightforward and simple but not always easy. Early on, the adjustments in thought, action, and behavior can seem counterintuitive and strange. Depending on the depth of your issues, the opening path can be bumpy.

Don't worry. Keep coming back. We did it, so can you. Our lives changed for the better, so can yours. Keep coming back. No matter what. Keep coming back.

No matter the specifics of your repetitive behaviors, keep coming back. The more recovery, the more collateral awareness and wellbeing.

How will you keep coming back?

"We call brothers and sisters who are similarly affected. Much to our amazement, we discover that they welcome our call."

Mindfulness

Mindfulness is the most important tool in my toolbox. The concept has different meanings for different people. For me it means being as present and awake as possible every moment of the day—the first sip of coffee in the morning, hearing laughter, the sun peeking through clouds, dropping into meditation, finishing a workout. Catching my lover's eye.

When in my disease, I was blind much of the time. Now I try to notice what I've missed. Sometimes it's effortless, and sometimes it feels impossible. But I keep coming back to the present when I stray. That's the important thing.

Present here and now: that's the state I was trying to avoid all those years trapped in harmful behaviors. I was trying to escape the present. There was too much pain, regret, and damage there.

Now, mindfulness is like a spotlight guiding me through the maze of life's ups and downs.

For example, it's only natural that I worry about my kids. I can lapse into *what ifs* when I'm scared of the future and *if only* when I'm regretting past mistakes. One thought leads to another—incessantly.

I want to control their every move because I will find it intolerable to live with all the catastrophic consequences I'm imagining.

How could I have been so stupid?
What if she just doesn't come home tonight!

He's going to lose his license!
Then what?
I can't believe I did it again.
Why didn't I check his pockets!

Staying in the moment can be difficult, but obsessing is worse.

There's no getting around it: the only things I can get a handle on are the ones right in front of me, and even they can be elusive.

Everything else is a distraction, or worse—an escape. Here's a slogan I try to keep in mind:

Don't do today's work tomorrow.
Don't do tomorrow's work today.

All I have is this immediate sliver of time. It's the only sliver that matters, the only place I'm truly alive.

What's in this moment for you?

"You should sit in meditation for twenty minutes every day—unless you are too busy; then you should sit for an hour."
— Zen Proverb

There are many ways to meditate other than traditional meditation practices. As James Finley suggests in *The Contemplative Heart:*

> "A contemplative practice is any act, habitually entered into with your whole heart, as a way of awakening, deepening, and sustaining a contemplative experience of the inherent holiness of the present moment. Your practice might be meditation such as sitting motionless in silence, attentive and awake to the abyss-like nature of each breath. Your practice might be simple, heartfelt prayer, slowly reading the scriptures, gardening, baking bread, writing or reading poetry, drawing or painting, or perhaps running or taking long, slow walks to no place in particular."

In meditation, I try to surrender my delusional belief that I am omniscient, saving me from my inextricable bondage to myself—to control, to illusions of my own grandeur, to any pretense that I am in charge.

I leave my human concerns, regrets, and foibles behind to touch the endless flow that preceded me and will follow long after me. I have nothing to do with it. It supersedes any effect I might have upon it. To be a part of it, even briefly, I will set myself aside and enter the flow willingly, let go, and give myself over to its unknowing.

What if every conscious breath is a meditation?

CHAPTER 8

Rebuilding

"Don't count the days, make the days count."
— Muhammad Ali

There's only one thing that changes in recovery, and that's *everything.*

Honesty, openness, willingness, and other basic principles have changed my view of the world so profoundly that it seems like the world itself has changed, and very much for the better.

Yet, every day I think of reasons not to use my tools.

I don't have time.
I miss my old ways.
It seems like a lot of trouble?
What if it doesn't work?
The cravings are too intense!
I'm not sure it's worth it.

Then I remember how much time and money I squandered on my addictions and behaviors—the risks I took, the loneliness, the rejection, the frustration of trying to control others and the hurts inflicted and absorbed.

Now I balance these against saving my life and building a future. Recovery's return on investment is exponential!

As I progressed, I gave up many of my connections to the past: old friends, old habits, old stomping grounds, old ways of thinking.

The goal was to replace them with healthier choices. I shifted focus from old distractions to the truth of my new reality.

Now, after some time in recovery, it's simpler and more ingrained. I know that if I get distracted by fear or the frustrations of daily life, I can be susceptible to relapse. I put those concerns in the back seat. I stay in the front, driving with my eyes on the road ahead.

Recovery helps me with emotional awareness and balance and is always along for the ride. It packs light and always fits.

What do you want to change?

Progress Not Perfection

My father used to say, "Do little things well and greater things will come, asking to be done." It was his favorite aphorism.

He was a piano teacher, and it was his constant refrain to his students. It spoke to his method of practice and competency.

Sometimes I hear the tiny critic in my head whispering,

You'll never get this right.
You don't need recovery.
You've been at this for months.
Aren't you cured yet?
Come on, enough is enough.
You're not sure it's even working.

Repetitive tendencies honed over lifetimes are stubborn, resilient, and not easily altered.

Ceasing substances or behaviors is one thing; staying clear of them day after day is quite another.

Cleansing the body of our physical attachments is just the beginning. Resisting a behavior is similarly only the beginning. Redirecting the mind can take years.

I couldn't have quit alcohol or learned to manage my co-dependent tendencies without constant repetition. My old defaults were repetitive and forceful. I needed something equally repetative and forceful to oppose, understand and eventually replace them.

In 1970, while an employee of Gordon Training International, Noel Birch proposed the following theory of learning new skills called the four stages of competence.

These four stages of learning are fundamental in the process of acquiring new skills in all areas of life, including recovery.

1. **Unconscious incompetence (Ignorance)** – At the beginning, we don't know and we don't know we don't know. We are weighed down by ignorance, denial, and self-will. We must be awakened to our problems or deficits before we can learn new skills to solve them.

2. **Conscious incompetence (Awareness)** – Now we know we have a deficit, but we aren't sure how to fix it yet. We try things until we find a skill set that suits our need and dive in. Trial and error—making mistakes is part of learning new skills.

3. **Conscious competence (Learning)** – Now we're cookin'! We are actively engaged in learning the new skills. Now we concentrate and practice, practice, practice. "Wax on, wax off."

4. **Unconscious competence (Mastery)** – After much hard work we have honed the solution to our problem. It's in our bones: automatic, baked in, and cellular. Now we can share and teach it to others.

We might believe we are done here. "Okay, I got these recovery skills down and they are instinctive—I'm cured, recovered. I don't need active recovery anymore. Adios, muchachos!"

But no! Addictive impulses are lifelong; they are never cured, only managed. Skill repetition is crucial. Those of us who have been in recovery for a while know that we must treat our disease every day, the same way that we eat every day and sleep every day to nourish and restore ourselves.

We remain humble in the face of the knowledge acquired. Humility is crucial. The moment we are convinced that we are cured is the moment we are the most vulnerable.

Do we do any of this perfectly? NO! We are human, we make mistakes. It's impossible to do it perfectly, but we can continue *persistently*, gathering knowledge and insights every day along the way.

Most addicts who stay sober use recovery tools for the rest of their lives. And why not? It's heartening, fun, and new friendships abound. We begin living a new experience in life.

And when things get rough or shaky, there is usually someone sane who can pull us out of the pit we've been digging.

How can you stay consistant and reach out when necessary?

Recovery works,
it just doesn't work your way.

Addicts have a propensity to be grandiose and self-important. We may not like ourselves much, but we're all we think about.

It's all my fault. I should have been a better parent.
I have to rescue them, or they won't survive.
I can handle it on my own.
I'm the best person for that job.
I'm the worst person in the world.

This is where the tool of humility comes in handy. Humility doesn't mean weak or meek or submissive. It means we understand our place in our surroundings. It means we don't take ourselves too seriously.

I was so used to rejecting direction from others that it was a real challenge to accept even the gentlest suggestion. Defense and defiance don't die easily.

I had to be desperate before I could let go of my defiance, and that's how it was when I started recovery. I was so desperate after a lifetime of pain that I was willing to listen and do whatever was asked of me. My desperation was greater than my resistance.

But as I started to feel better, I became more like my old self. I started nitpicking, criticizing this, and judging that. Then these little nitpicks started turning into resentments.

After a while, I realized a part of me was defaulting to prideful old ways of thinking: judging, separating, resenting, holding grudges, and projecting what I hated about myself onto others.

My mind was sabotaging my intention to get well. It was creating any excuse to get back on the couch with a can of beer or a glass of single malt and a bowl mixed nuts. My addict self was alive and well.

When I shared that with my sponsor, he told me that he went through the same thing early on, and still did sometimes.

So did lots of others.

Giving up judgments and old ideas isn't easy, but as Douglas Adams suggested, "It's more important to be happy than to be right." It wasn't my usual way, but it's the way that works.

Do you want to be happy or right?

"Everything you've ever wanted is sitting on the other side of fear."
— George Addair

I was afraid of my father—he had a temper.
I was afraid of my mother—her emotional
neediness.
I was afraid of the swimming pool—I was chubby.
I was afraid of my early childhood diseases—they
threatened me.
I was afraid of school—I was dyslexic and didn't
do well.
I was afraid to go to sleep—tomorrow scared me.
I was afraid of people—I was socially awkward.
I was afraid of dating—I didn't know how.
I was afraid for myself—I felt lost and clueless.
I was afraid of getting married—I didn't understand
love.
I was afraid of having children—I didn't know how
to be a parent.
I was afraid of my career—they would discover my
incompetence.
I was afraid to have strong opinions—I might be
wrong.
I was afraid to speak up for myself—I didn't deserve
it.
I was afraid to ask for what I wanted—I would be
rejected.
I was afraid to be myself—nobody would like me.
Fear, fear, fear, fear, fear

I was afraid of fear itself—what a frigging mess. I don't know how I got out of bed in the morning. I certainly never wanted to.

Here's the basic conundrum: fear is a rational survival mechanism, but it can often be irrational. It's hard to tell the difference because the feeling is the same either way.

As fear was my constant companion, I learned to hide from it behind alcohol, food, fantasy, TV, chocolate, sex, and the compulsion to fix others. These were automatic responses that helped me dilute its intensity.

Fear stopped me from doing much I wanted to do, and infected everything I did do. I constantly felt weighed down by a blanket of foreboding that had to be overcome to accomplish anything at all.

It was exhausting!

The moment I took a drink, my fear abated. No wonder it felt so powerful. Alcohol was the solution to my problem.

It made me more fun, more creative, and more pleasant to be around. It provided a freedom that I had never known before.

Similarly, butting into your business, telling you what to do, or trying to fix your problems distracted me from my own fears. Instead of obsessing about myself, I would obsess about you. When you wouldn't listen, righteous indignation would act as yet another handy distraction.

Ultimately, however, these magical solutions morphed into my biggest fear of all: a fear of servitude to forces I couldn't control. That's when the bottom came up and smacked me back to reality.

If I listen, act, seek recovery, and face myself, then I can start seeing the difference between rational and irrational fear.

I can explore places, people, ideas, spiritual connections, growth, sustainability, and other things I never imagined.

What do you fear?

This too shall pass.

I am intimidated by the breadth and depth of my insatiable desire.

It's stealthy and ambushes my best intentions. Sometimes all that exists is this desire—palpable, immutable, and unquenchable. My instincts and habits, overindulged over the years, compel and reignite old behaviors.

Buy that. Overspend.
Get him under control.
Work, work, work!
Just one drink this time.
Escape! This is too hard.
I'm going to eat all of it.
I can't resist!

With every attack of desire, there's a choice: I either give in or I don't. When it happens to me, I try to pause, ground myself, and recognize that I'm under assault. I can't stop the desire, so I let it come—and I let it go. It arises, endures, then fades away.

It always goes. It fades away a moment at a time if I let it. At first, this letting go process can seem endless, even impossible at times, but slowly the compulsive urges soften and become less powerful.

After practicing for a time, the whole sequence shortens and becomes less emotionally charged. Now it's more like a reminder of what used to be.

Urges do pass if we face them, endure their momentary grip, and picture the consequences that could come if we give in.

I saw my consequences in my son's eyes. All I have to do now is remember that moment. By the time that memory has passed, the urge has passed too, and I'm sober for another moment of another sober day.

How can you accept the urge without acting on it?

I'M GOING TO EAT IT ALL...(EVEN IF IT KILLS ME!)

ADDICTION IS A FAMILY DISEASE

Don't stay hooked on their story.

One of the traps in recovery, especially for those of us obsessing about our addicts, is clinging to their story. The goal in recovery, for a co-dependent like me, is to focus on my own life, not someone else's.

When I began recovery, I couldn't help focusing on those with issues around me. The thought of paying attention to my own life seemed impossible. There was simply too much to do trying to solve their problems.

It felt like I was stuck in a loop, and I was. The loop was my own addiction to fixing them.

As we, the friends and family of the addict, come into recovery, we tend to tell our addict's story repeatedly, hoping that in the telling we will stumble over a solution.

We keep telling the story to try to process our own confused emotions, our anger, sadness, shame, or guilt. We're trying to find solid ground and understand how things got so screwed up.

Those feelings can be so raw and visceral that it's hard to experience anything else.

As we move forward in the recovery process and talk with others, we experience a gradual internal shift. It happens automatically.

The old story and the emotions around it dissipate and are replaced with new ideas about what we can do for ourselves. Our own repressed life force starts emerging.

We begin to stand on our own as we detach from our unhealthy attachment to them. Our obsession with them cracks, and we peek out into the wide world again.

It doesn't happen overnight, but it does happen. We slowly realize their story may not change—but ours can.

The same evolution is true of the addict. The more they stay stuck in their own story, the guilt and shame they feel, the slower their recovery.

What's your new story?

Checkup From The Neck Up

I go to my general practitioner every year for a checkup. He's thorough, poking and prodding, lots of tests, EKG, blood work, pressure, weight, and reflexes.

I try to exercise every day, eat well, mostly, and avoid old default habits like smoking, sugar, caffeine, and alcohol. But I still need checkups. So does my car.

In recovery we need checkups too, sometimes daily—more often on difficult days. We can do a lot of them ourselves. The ability to take one's own physical, spiritual, and emotional checkup or inventory is a key to staying away from addictive behaviors.

Am I feeling anxious? If so, why?
Have I been judgmental?
Have I hurt someone else?
Is it any of my business?
What's causing these feelings?

An introspective inventory is the antidote to denial. It's being attentive to the moment.

When we leave our old habits behind and begin life in the present, we begin to see and feel things that escaped our consciousness before. We're no longer numb to our feelings or blind to our actions.

That means we can stop and take stock whenever questions or feelings arise. If things aren't going well, am I part of the problem? If so, what part? What can I do about it?

If I look at what's going on in my head and my heart, I can address the problem with confidence rather than escaping into substances or behaviors.

Maybe I can begin working on a solution. Maybe I can see that it's not even my problem to solve.

When disturbed, how can you pause and look inside?

Reality is life on life's terms.

Reality isn't what I think it is, what I want it to be, or what I hope it could be. Reality is what it is. It has no character of its own other than what I give it through my perceptions, thoughts, and emotions.

In my disease, I deluded myself into believing that I could change, mitigate, and/or escape my current reality. In truth, I only momentarily changed my perception of it. Once that perception faded, reality was often worse than when I left it.

So, here's an example. Let's say my daughter has some issues with eating, purging, eating, and purging. I am co-dependent with her. My addiction wants to help her get better, so I jump through every hoop in the known universe to ensure the outcome I so desperately desire.

I ask her in passing, "Are you still going to that eating program and seeing the therapist?"

She replies, "Un hun, sure," retreating into her bedroom.

"Great," I say over the click of the door lock. I walk away feeling a little better than I did a minute ago.

But has anything changed? Nothing really, except my perception of her problem has changed incrementally. The fact is I don't know if she's telling me the truth. She could still be eating and purging.

For all I know, her problem could be getting worse. I could check to see if she's still in therapy, but she's over eighteen. By law, she's an adult. Her therapist won't talk to me, and it's none of my business anyway.

I just want to feel better and assuage my fears. I want her to get better so I feel better.

Things have not changed at all. Her reality seems the same and my reality with her is no different.

But by asking and receiving this half-baked assurance, I let my perception become momentarily distorted for the better. Hope springs eternal, the old saying goes. But is that always wise?

The feeling didn't last long. I recognized the distortion dipped in wishful thinking. I reminded myself that I have no control over her reality and very little over my own.

This momentary relief was a quick trick of perception. Reality changed not one bit. Only my hope for a different reality.

In recovery, we learn to be in acceptance of reality, as profoundly unsettling as it might be sometimes. UGH!

What reality is bothering you?

No Matter What Club

At first, abstinence from your repetitive behaviors seems almost impossible. You feel alone, isolated, and misunderstood. Your addiction may seem to be your only lifeline. If attached to an addict, you can't imagine not fixing him or her or them.

How can I even imagine living without it?
What will happen if I do give it up?
Will I completely deconstruct?
Will it be painful?
What will I do instead?
Who would I even be? No one, I fear.
How can I face myself without it?
How can I even start to recover?
Will it even work?
Do I dare start today?

Start with us. We in recovery are waiting for you. Come home to this new way of living. Your seat is reserved. Welcome! We will show you how it works. You don't have to know anything or do anything to walk through the door.

No one will judge you. We are your brothers and sisters. We will go out of our way to help you as others have helped us. It's our duty, our obligation, our enduring legacy, and our joy.

We know what you are going through. We've been through it many times. We understand, we empathize, and we offer solutions you may not have considered or encountered before.

It takes courage to join us at your most vulnerable, but in this vulnerability resides some solutions to your problems. It's the opportunity to see your truth clearly and rebuild those lost parts of yourself. Stop living in the family disease of addiction and start living in the family solution of recovery.

Begin to grieve the loss and acceptance of what could have been, what was hoped for and dreamt of. This is not easy but essential. Recalibrate expectations, get real, get well, and get ready for the rest of your life. Create new hopes and dreams grounded in the truth of your current life and the immense possibilities it offers.

Become a member of the No Matter What Club. No matter what.

> *I will no longer participate in my harmful behaviors.*
> *I will no longer try to fix my addict.*
> *I pledge this to myself.*
> *Life is not easy; there will be numerous ups and downs, even extremes of divorce, death, illness, bankruptcy, and many other difficulties inherent in the human condition, but regardless of the pain or loss or harm done I will not default to my obsessive or addictive behaviors.*
> *No Matter What!*
> *I won't do it perfectly, but I will do my best.*

Have you had ENOUGH?

"We've been through It many times. We understand, we empathise and we offer solutions..."

Touching My Own Emptiness

I always admired people with purpose, people who had passion, people who knew what they wanted and were willing to pay the price to have it. I never understood that kind of commitment, so I just drifted and attached to the nearest thing I could find.

I attached to my profession because I was afraid of poverty, and I was successful at it. It was intense, high-pressure work, and it mattered to a lot of people. But it never resonated deep down. Nothing did, really.

I tried to change myself to fit every situation. I was like a bird skimming the treetops, never diving down to discover the world in the forest below or climbing to the clouds. Most of the time, I was miserable.

I tried therapy from time to time and got some momentary relief. But I never knew who I was or what motivated me. I tried to love, but I didn't know how. I let my loved ones down.

How can I be true to others if I don't even know myself?
Will I reach the end of my life never meeting the guy who lived it?

When I set aside my addictive behaviors, I could see how I had been relying on them, other people, and outside distractions to define who I was. I was the guy who drank. The son who ran. The father who controlled. The husband who failed.

I felt hollow, like there was no me there.

Curiosity showed me I was wrong about that. Now that I could take a clear look at myself and how I fit into the world, I began to ask, "What's this me I am observing, the I am I? What does this me want to be, regardless of outside influences?'

Simple curiosity about how the universe works and how I work in the universe is like a spotlight. It illuminates parts of me that were hidden, parts I couldn't see, parts I feared observing.

Dr. Mark Epstein summed it up beautifully in his book, *Going to Pieces Without Falling.* "Only by learning how to touch the ground of our own emptiness can we feel whole again."

I have found this seeming paradox to be true. There is no judgment in emptiness, no expectation, no criticism, no pain, only an open road to be the person you want to be, the person you were meant to be, the person you really are.

It reminds me that I still have places to explore, that lots of things are possible: leaving the past in the past, leaving the future to its own devices, and an untold depth in each sliver of time I choose to inhabit.

How will it feel to set down what you're carrying?

Carry the Message

Addicts are like pigeons in a couple of ways. They make messes wherever they go but often carry important messages.

Recovery programs work in large part because an addict trying to get well will generally be more receptive to the message delivered by another addict. While ignoring doctors, family, and friends, the conversation with a recovering addict is stickier and holds more weight.

They have been there.
They know the way out.
They understand.

"The best way to find yourself is to lose yourself in the service of others." That's a great Gandhi quote, though it's unclear whether the mahatma ever really said it.

For self-centered addicts, it hits home. A critical component in recovery is shifting from "self" to "other." Being willing to help others, we help ourselves stay sober.

That happened to me too.
I know that feeling.
It's like that for everybody.
You're not alone!

It's just the opposite for relatives and friends who have been selfless in support of others' addictions. They have dedicated themselves to controlling, helping, rescuing, and saving others at their own expense.

Their job in recovery is to *stop* losing themselves in others and focus on their own health and happiness. They learn to let go and allow their addicts to find their own path.

As a loved one, I learned that there are two kinds of business—my business and none of my business.

In either case, carrying and sharing the message of renewal is key to getting better and recovering our own sense of value and purpose.

Do you need to give more or give less?

"Addicts are like pigeons; they shit all over the place, but can also carry the message."

CHAPTER 9

Responsibility, Restitution, and Restoration

"And now that you don't have to be perfect, you can be good. Is that it?"

— John Steinbeck, *East of Eden*

Recovery is a grow-up accelerator, turbocharging a more realistic and manageable present-day reality.

I have learned to take care of my parts that are afraid and feel threatened—vulnerable and unprotected. Those parts that acted irrationally and got me in trouble.

I take things slower now, am more considerate of my fellows, and have rejoined the community as a healthy productive member.

Recovery is not for those of us who need it or want it. It's for those of us who do it. Luckily, we don't have to do it perfectly. Certainly, I never have.

That said, we forge ahead every day imperfectly.

1. We admit we have problems we can't endure any more.
2. We admit we are powerless and seek help.
3. We turn things over to more competent hands.
4. *Hands that are not ours!*
5. We sort out our flawed thinking.
6. We deep-dive into our history and the behaviors that marred it.
7. We identify our character limitations and begin addressing them.
8. We make amends to those we have hurt.

9. We commit to daily inventory to assess progress and setbacks.
10. We take time every day to rest, reflect, and contemplate.
11. We help others and follow healthy principles for living.

What's stopping you?

Addicts treat loneliness with isolation.

As our addiction wounds us, we tend to crawl under a bush and snarl at anyone who tries to help. Addiction is a disease of secrecy and loneliness. Recovery works when we give up our secrets.

Addiction is a lonely business; recovery is not. We learn to take contrary actions and reach out for help. For many, this is a revolutionary concept and often difficult to do—the phone can feel impossibly heavy—the instinct to hide and isolate is so powerful, especially when we are dominated by guilt, shame, and regret.

Who would want to talk to me?
I don't want to bother her.
He's so together and I'm such a mess.
She seems like a big shot.
He won't even answer.
I'm not talking; it won't help anyway.
Ugh! This is so hard.

Yes, it was hard at first, but every time I got over myself and reached out to another in recovery, I felt a little stronger. I still do, and it almost always helps both of us. A problem shared is a problem halved.

Sometimes just leaving a text or phone message is enough to take the edge off if I'm feeling antsy or upset. When people call me, I don't need to offer advice. I just try to be a good listener.

It's not safe for me to be alone with my ego, my thoughts, or my pain. Contact counts. We help each other get better.

Who have you spoken with today?

Actions Speak Louder

I make my bed every morning on waking.
I do not use or drink one day at a time.
I don't tell you what to do or how to do it.
I mind my own business.
I wait for you to ask before offering help.
I do not spend beyond my means, I do not gamble,
I do not steal.
I am honest and truthful.
I don't ask the impossible.
I am a better friend in divorce than I was a husband
in marriage.
I am responsible.
I am consistent and take care of business.
I am rebuilding my character.
I am more self-aware and adjust as needed.
I work on my recovery every day.
I turn over control to something greater than
myself.

As I recover, well-intended action has become my keystone. Without it, the edifice of my recovery will crumble. Along with healthy thinking, healthy action starts to tell my new story. If I wander or slip, I now possess enough self-awareness to notice.

I can feel it inside. It's like food poisoning. It doesn't take long to know something is wrong. I might feel sad, uneasy, off-kilter, or even sick at heart. I already have too much recovery to ignore the signs.

So, I take stock, inventory my feelings and their causes, talk to others, reason things out, and get back on track. This I do moment to moment, day to day, until it becomes automatic—a new way of living—repetition is essential, striving to be better than the day before.

What's working for you?

Amends are more than apologies.

Get well and get ready for life beyond addiction. It's time we put on our big boy/girl pants and fess up. It's time to take responsibility without blame or equivocation.

This is where the rubber meets the road. This is where we bare our souls, admit where we are at fault, and express the truth of our actions.

Wow! Talk about a palate cleanser.

In this dance of addiction, there have been thousands of apologies strewn about carelessly—auto-apologies. Apologies in the moment, apologies to get folks off our backs, apologies to avoid arguments and conflict, apologies for temporary relief, and apologies to seek forgiveness. They are often self-serving and mostly a dime a dozen. They never added up to much. Sorry, sorry, sorry!

> *That was the last time, I swear.*
> *Please, please, give me another chance.*
> *I'm sorry I interfered. Please forgive me.*
> *I promise I'll change.*

Amends are quite different. They are acts of surrendering to our own limitations and making the solemn promise not to impose those limitations on others.

I tried for years to talk myself back into others' good graces, to salvage some credibility, but the more I talked, the less they listened—the less they believed.

I finally realized that I can't change what others think of me. I can only change myself. The people I've failed may come to trust me again, or they may not. It's up to them. Nobody has an obligation to forgive me.

I can only be willing to do whatever I can to mend the relationship, and mending means amending—changing my thinking and my actions.

What would a real amends mean to you?

"...humility and the conscious knowledge of what we have done and who we have hurt should be crystal clear to us."

A wall is a wall;
a boundary is a wall with a door.

My recovery is the most important guard-rail in my life. Without it, I might end up in the gutter. Without it, nothing else works as it should. Without it, I would return to a very miserable way of life.

But how do I protect my recovery? By setting appropriate boundaries and saying *yes* and *no* and meaning it.

No thanks. I don't do that anymore.
You go ahead. I'm getting ready for work.
I can't make that choice for you. You decide.

My efforts to date have given me the tools to be discerning, not judgmental; clear, not confused; self-determining, not manipulated.

The clouds have parted enough that all the old triggers do not attack with the same emotional intensity as in the past.

Now I get to pick and choose what I let in. Things, people, and situations that are toxic, I leave out. They are no longer welcome. I have learned to live without their incessant drama.

The trajectory of my experience is less dependent on what's on the other side of the wall. I no longer depend on it to fulfill my needs. I have strengthened my resolve, tapped into my intuition, and reignited my common sense.

"Who looks outside dreams, who looks inside
awakes." — Carl Jung

I am finally cured of any grandiose illusions that I can fix all the distortions, pain, and stupidity outside that used to drive me mad. I leave them be, on the other side. I let go to have peace of mind.

I am now living a more skilled life. I care less about more and more about less.

How can you feel safe today?

Think Less, Be More

Thought hygiene is critical to recovery and life in general. My thinker is not always trustworthy. Sometimes it thinks it's in charge, fomenting havoc by being unhelpful, self-accusing, regretful, worrying, anxious-making, and sometimes even debilitating.

I can be driving along on my merry way and have a thought that, if entertained for any amount of time, might drive me to distraction or depression.

> *If I hadn't done that,*
> *If only I had done that!*
> *I can't do that.*
> *If I had done that, he'd still be alive.*
> *I shouldn't have said that.*
> *I'm so afraid of what's next.*
> *I'm not good enough.*
> *I'll never get it right!*
> *I'm such a loser.*

If my brain were a hard drive, all these thoughts would be sleeper malware, ready to download into my consciousness when I least expect it. Ruminating is like running endless loops in hell.

For most of my life, I entertained these kinds of thoughts— self-doubting thoughts. I believed them or fought with or tried to change them, but they always prevailed—constantly buffering.

With practice, I learned to look at my inner dialogue for what it is—not very trustworthy. Some of the thoughts still arise, but now my response to them is quite different. I don't take them to heart anymore. Most are exaggerated and many untrue.

Now I can choose to stand back, notice their attack, ground myself, replace them, and get on with my day.

Much of addiction centers in the mind – Stinkin' Thinkin'. Learning to mitigate this harmful self-talk is one of the central pillars of renewed health and wellness.

What are you saying to yourself?

"Ruminating is like running laps in hell."

CHAPTER 10

The New Constants

What Doesn't Kill Me

When I was trapped in my own addiction and those of my loved ones, it often felt like I was rushing toward a waterfall in a flimsy canoe.

It was a long drop to a rocky bottom, notorious for shattering many lives.

What a relief to live through it! But after climbing out of the water, checking for broken bones, and surveying my battered canoe, there were some obvious questions.

Why did I survive? And what now?

Why was I spared while many others are not? And where do I go from here? Oh, and how do I avoid the next waterfall?

I got my first glimmer of an answer when I heard a friend say he felt lucky to be an alcoholic. It sounded unhinged until I came to understand it myself.

The life I'm enjoying today wouldn't be possible without the failures and tragedies that taught me how to live it. If I'm grateful to be here and alive, I must express some gratitude for how I got here.

By the time you read this, I will be seventy-eight or older, if I'm still around. I'm stronger now than I ever was—not physically, that strength is waning, but mentally and spiritually.

"What doesn't kill me, makes me stronger," goes the well-worn Friedrich Nietzsche aphorism.

But for all his nihilistic gloom, the philosopher had a point. What if the plunge down that waterfall is what finally woke me up—woke me up to my life—woke me up to better ways of living my life? What if I couldn't have progressed any other way?

Marcus Aurelius practiced this principle time and time again, obstacle after obstacle, thousands of years ago:

> "The impediment to action advances action.
> What stands in the way becomes the way."

I try not to forget this and other important lessons. They inspire me to be proactive—to keep plugging along even when new challenges present themselves.

They're like indelible markers, always there to remind me how far I've come. I need them because I still have those survivor's questions. Why me? And what now?

Where is your canoe headed?

Forgiveness of Self

I couldn't imagine forgiving myself. Self-punishment felt like what I deserved. It was my penance.

Forgiveness of others was obvious. The resentments I carried against them were poisoning me. I had to let them go—forgive them for my own good.

But forgiveness for myself was harder. I couldn't even imagine what it would look like. My failings were too obvious, too hurtful, and too numerous.

I deserve all the punishment I get.
How can I live with myself?
They might let me off the hook, but I can't.
My shame, guilt, and unforgiveness feel right.

In a self-seeking way, this pity party kept me attached to those I loved who didn't want me in their lives anymore. The only way I could retain my attachment to them was to hope they would take pity on me and come back into my life. This form of self-pity is its own addiction, and it's very unattractive.

Self-forgiveness came slowly.

With help and time in recovery, I stopped beating myself up when I realized that I was looping in and out of the same kind of thinking that dominated my addiction days. Just as I did in early recovery, I had to accept, surrender, and stop fighting.

ADDICTION IS A FAMILY DISEASE

When I finally offered amends for things I'd done, I didn't ask for forgiveness. Yet surprisingly, often it was offered to me.

The best I will ever be is human. There is tremendous grace in forgiveness. When part of me feels like it needs to be punished, I try to remember that my addiction was punishment enough.

Martin Luther King counseled that "Forgiveness is not an occasional act; it is a constant attitude."

What can you forgive in yourself?

Imagining More

My addiction issues don't interest me much anymore. Living in the presence of recovery does. My addictions used to be the center of attention, dominating my imaginings. Now they are peripheral, circling the outer circumference of what is now a reordered life.

When I finally entered recovery, I did it with intention. I was willing to learn, I put my ego aside for the most part, and I buckled down to work. The ten years since have been an amazing ride. Not unlike life itself, there have been ups and downs, but my resolve to live a better life has been steadfast.

Desperation compelled me to change.
I asked for help and accepted it.
I stayed, I stay, I look forward to staying.
I re-commit every day.
I have embraced this new way of life.

For a very long time I couldn't imagine that these things would be part of my everyday life.

I'm in loving relationships.
I'm writing this book.
I have two jobs I enjoy.
I'm in service to others.
I'm not afraid anymore.
I'm a sober alcoholic.
I'm a recovering co-dependent.
I stay out of others' business.
I don't try to manage anyone but myself.

Where does your imagination take you?

Gratitude fills the space that is wanting.

I'm coming to the end of who I thought I was. I am free from what is no longer true. Every day I have a reprieve, and every day I remind myself of the immense gratitude I feel as a result.

Each morning, I list a few of the things that I appreciate, and once started the list inevitably grows. I am grateful for:

Waking up
Morning Coffee
My little cactus garden
The view from my balcony
My Partner
Evening walks
Simple things
Peace of mind

As I feel the emotional impact of these gratitudes, I feel full, replete, and content. Gratitude has become one of the constants in my life.

Sometimes I forget. I regress into anger, acquisition, escape, controlling, fixing, worrying, and wallowing in gloom. They feel awful enough to nudge me back to gratitude, which is a much happier place to inhabit.

It's almost impossible to feel angry and grateful at the same time. In gratitude, there is very little room for negative emotions.

So, I shift quickly back to gratitude for people, for electricity, for air, water and food, flowers, ants, and mixed nuts. I remind myself again and again that I have been granted another chance to make better use of myself.

As the old defaults wane, they are replaced by curiosity, empathy, imagination, understanding, awareness, empowerment, and a compelling sense of oneness and awe that supersedes thought, resides in spirit, and becomes more and more indelible as it expands.

"For my part, I am almost contented just now, and very thankful. Gratitude is a divine emotion: it fills the heart, but not to bursting; it warms it, but not to fever."
— Charlotte Brontë

What are you grateful for today?

Let's Review:
The Four Stages of Recovery

1. Survival — Physical Sobriety

We have discussed this first stage in the opening chapters.

If you are a person living in the disease of addiction, you know it well. It's compulsive, driven by forces way beyond your control. You are trapped in your own addiction or the addiction of a loved one.

Nothing is normal—much is troubled. You feel isolated. There is no way out. You don't know how you will survive another day.

In this stage much is swept under the rug. Denial, magical thinking, and small bits of hope try to ward off the inevitable crash that is coming.

Your first recovery intervention might look something like this:

You:
Stop being the cause of your own suffering.
Make a phone call to the recovery program.
Talk to a friend instead of taking a pill.
Stop going to Vegas and join Gambler's Anonymous.
Clear the junk food from your kitchen.
Stop giving advice to your pot-smoking kid.
Install porn restrictions on your computer and phone.
Mind your own business, even if you're right.
Stop your wine subscription.

Set a time limit for video gaming.
Work less and engage more with family and friends.
Create a budget to rein in spending and cut up credit cards.
Walk during the cocktail hour.

Here we are simply trying to create physical separation by interrupting the compulsive behavior. It's a big step. It implies that you see a truth that requires remediation.

"We are masters at fooling ourselves, denial, sweeping under the rug."

2. Sustainment/Security — Mental Sobriety

Once we transition from survival to sustainment, it means that we have accepted the radical act of recovery. We are no longer fighting the old daemons. Instead, we are trying to understand and replace them.

This is an action-packed, work-intensive stage that demands courage, resilience, and fortitude. In doing the work, we feel more and more secure every day as we commit to these new principles.

During this stage we may vacillate, wondering if the hard work is worth it. We may even slip, go out, or relapse. Then it's more important than ever to recommit. Ongoing recovery creates sustainability. With the help of our program, our mentors, and our friends, we constantly reassert our intention to prevail.

3. Surrender/Success — Emotional Sobriety

I once asked my sponsor, "How long do I have to do all this stuff like reading, writing, and going to meetings?"

He said, "Until you want to."

Once that moment comes, the moment of wanting recovery more than anything in the world, that is the tipping point, hopefully the point of no return.

Once on the other side, you feel it, that sense of surrender, that sense of giving up—giving in. They say that for an addict, surrender is a winning proposition. Finally, I have surrendered my old life, the life of harmful habits, to a new life of self-respect, truth, integrity, and all the other qualities that make living worthwhile.

It seems counterintuitive, but surrender propagates emotional sobriety, which leads in turn to a greater sense of all-around stability.

4. Serenity — Spiritual Sobriety

As a child, I loved standing in a doorway and pressing the back of my hands against the door jamb as hard as I could for as long as I could. Finally, exhausted I would step into open space, and like magic, my arms would start to rise as if gravity had taken a nap.

They rose like wings wanting to carry me upward into the clear blue sky. It was magical, inexplicable, and in it I sensed the freedom available to me if I sought it.

Recovery is very much the same. We push and push and push. Then finally we let go—and we float.

As we do, our experience in the world is transformed; we see and feel everything anew and now grow into the unexpected.

Our spirits rise into a new state of being—conscious, aware, and blessedly unencumbered.

CHAPTER 11

Spirit Rising

"There are, of course, the obvious benefits gained in the recovery process in terms of heightened levels of functioning. There is, as well, the spiritual metamorphosis arising from gazing long, and hard, in a compassionate, honest, and vulnerable manner into one's brokenness. In so doing one has the chance of discovering first hand the stuff of which the heart is made. In a no nonsense, down-to-earth kind of way, one hits bottom. In so doing one discovers that the bottom gives way to a yet deeper depth in which is granted an intimate experience of the divinity of ourselves as invincibly lovable and whole in all our fragmentation."

— **James Finley,**
The Contemplative Heart.

Came, came to, came to believe.

Came to believe what? *WHATEVER YOU WANT!*

The biggest misconception about many recovery programs, especially Twelve-Step programs, is that you must be religious or believe in God to get help, to recover—some God you don't understand, have no relationship with, or may not even like very much.

This single misconception probably turns more people away from recovery programs than any other obstacle. It kept me away for fifteen years while I white-knuckled sobriety on my own (not recommended, by the way).

When I finally came to recovery on my knees, it wasn't because I was praying—it was because I couldn't stand up. I was too broken, too bereft, too ashamed. Desperation brought me to recovery, not some promised spiritual awakening.

I had no idea what a spiritual awakening was and was sure that whatever it was, was not for me.

My sponsor encouraged me not to worry about God. He encouraged me to put all my old ideas about God, religion, and spirituality away—better yet, leave them behind. This was a new journey, and all I needed to start it were honesty, openness, and willingness. If I could do that, everything else would take care of itself.

As Rinpoche encouraged, "We must continue to open in the face of tremendous opposition."

What forces oppose you?

There are so many so-called gods in our world: science, industry, warfare, greed, money, politics, sex, outrage, media, possessions, addictions, religions, narcissism, selfishness, pride, ego, thought, co-dependence—and the beat goes on. They are all distractions and behaviors to bolster the importance of our manufactured selves. They give us the illusion of importance, strength, and entitlement. They separate us from one another, emphasizing our differences.

What happens when we subtract all these so-called gods from our focus? What if we can set them aside, even momentarily? What would be left? Would we be too afraid to look? Could we bear the nakedness of standing alone without these diversions to cover our shame, our regrets, and our fears? If we could stand naked with nothing to hide or defend, what then?

Perhaps then we could really feel the sacred sound humming within. Perhaps then we could touch something bigger than our fabricated concept of ourselves. Perhaps then, with everything else subtracted, we could see the unbending truth of our oneness and our connection, our breath, our being, and our deliverance from turmoil to an inexplicable realm of gentle surrender, higher consciousness, and peace.

Maybe this is the place where reconciliation exists. It was for me—as all my parts stopped brawling with one another and came together. Once this happened, I didn't have to fix myself anymore or fill the emptiness that I feared would defeat me. Instead, I tried to embrace everything just as it is.

It seems so obvious now. In this surrender to the unseen and the incomprehensible, I have established a relationship with the now-known source of my own understanding.

What is the source of your understanding?

As my addictions faded, and the compulsions emptied from me, space was opened for other things. I began to replace trauma, deregulation, anxiety, pain, obsession, hurt, anger, resentment, blame, control, attachment, judgment, worry, fear, and struggle with honesty, hope, courage, integrity, trust, willingness, humility, responsibility, brotherhood, perseverance, awareness, and being of service.

During such a monumental transformation, my spiritual experience shifted incrementally, stealthily, unknown to me. It happened of its own accord, as the cup of poison emptied and filled with fresh, cool spring water. It's not a stretch to suggest that if I drink water instead of poison, I might feel very different in mind, body, and spirit.

It's my choice now. This feeling that has enveloped me is mine alone. This feeling of wholeness inside, something bigger, kinder, more loving, and all-embracing that can hold and make space for all the paradoxes and contradictions of life—this is mine now and only needs to make sense to me.

If I want to name this new state of being, I'm free to call it whatever I want—like higher consciousness, peace of mind, universal energy, source, birds in flight, or the feeling of diving with dolphins as they circle in a rhythmic dance of belonging, welcoming my presence in their play—the feeling of being at one with them and myself, at one with the world, twenty feet below the surface, dancing, swimming, and rolling over and over in wonder so magical, quiet, and free, embraced by Mother Earth's offering of these congenial companions. And me just astounded by the warmth of this belonging and how embracing it feels—how sublime.

I don't have words enough for this feeling; I wish I did so I could properly share it with you. It's a feeling I have often now, this feeling of dancing with dolphins.

"Came, came to, came to believe."

The first and most important step in my recovery was to admit my powerlessness over the forces of addiction that consumed me. Likewise, the most important step for me concerning the addicts in my life was to admit my powerlessness over fixing them. In either case, the invitation was for me to turn my perceived power (that wasn't working anyway) to something, anything, greater than myself.

I cannot fathom the infinite. I have no idea who or what is in charge. It doesn't matter as long as it's not me. At first, I didn't understand this principle because I was acting as if I was the boss. Ha!

I had just seen the film *Gravity*, so I admitted that gravity was more powerful than me. I remembered dislocating my shoulder while kayaking, so water pressure was clearly more powerful than me.

Finally, I admitted that much of what goes on in the world, in nature, in life, is more powerful than me. I am now humbled by the reality of my own relativity.

This very recognition was a dawning of an awareness that gifted me with a great sense of relief. I was free of being responsible for all the problems in the world. I stopped trying to change the past, change reality, change others, or predict the future. In doing so, I had a lot more spare time to focus on whatever was presented in the moment. I'm reminded of the aphorism "There are two kinds of business: my business and none of my business."

A huge weight was lifted. It was a necessary humbling, a right sizing. Finally, I reached the emotional and intellectual understanding that it was time to do things differently. The first step was to finally admit my powerlessness and surrender to it.

Do you still think you're in charge?

Release from the desperate obsession of addiction in any form is a unique phenomenon. There is something wonderful about watching a kite in the sky. That feeling of uplift is no different in recovery. We might call it relief—being set free, liberated, emancipated—our spirit soars into a new understanding and appreciation.

The only way to understand it is to imagine that you have been utterly powerless and imprisoned by your behaviors for much of your life. Imagine when the jailer opens the final gate and sends you out into the sunlight, closing the gate behind you! It's a renewal, a rebirth, a new lease on life.

To not experience it in your spirit would be almost impossible. In a singular life, this experience is an epiphany of colossal proportions that expands infinitely as one stays committed to the path.

Recovery is much like an open-book test. There are no rules, regulations, or restrictions. You get to do the test your way—developing your own relationship with health, wellbeing, and spirit unhindered by convention.

Evolving spirit is not a requirement of recovery programs, only a suggestion, and often eventually a byproduct. Let whatever will happen, happen organically. Don't force it; you can't. It's not the way it works. Don't sweat it—*all will be well.*

How can you let go?

For many, this spiritual connection, whatever it may be for each individual person, becomes a guiding light in the progression of recovery, along with new principles of daily life and service to others.

What I have experienced is that something has entered my life as I seek it and allow it. I believe I always sought this feeling, wished for it, yearned even, but could never overcome the distractions and compulsions of my life long enough to feel its ongoing presence.

I would only have moments of connection that I never named but were there nonetheless—a moment watching a sunset, the smell of earth after a summer rain, the feeling of being cared for. I felt it while watching a flock of birds swirl in unison, thousands arching, twisting, and turning altogether, guided by the hand of nature's invisible conductor.

I've heard it in the sound of children's laughter at the playground, sitting in the woods, peaceful and quiet, or watching storm clouds stream over the ridge line, rushing over the valley, I felt it as sunlight pierced the gaps like spotlights illuminating yuccas on the desert floor below. And perching on boulders under the canopy of the lone pinion tree with my best friend and our young boys, resting on top of Whale Mountain as we watched the desert terrain stretching to infinity in nature's full array, marveling at the profound wonder of it all.

What could all these things be? They would affect me so. How could I hold these feelings forever without forgetting? But forget I often did, until now.

Now I don't forget. I remember. I yearn to inhabit this terrain forever. It has been gifted to me. I don't understand it. I accept it with open arms, and I don't betray it. It has never betrayed me—comforting even in my darkest moments. I don't know what it is, but I do know *it is*. Some call it the "Is-ness."

I don't have to call it anything. It calls me.

What's calling you?

The End

Art Dielhenn, CPCC

Art is a certified career coach living in Los Angeles. In 1999 he founded Los Angeles Coaching to work with creative professionals and those in correlated industries.

Prior to coaching, he enjoyed a fulfilling, three-decade career directing both public and network commercial television.

Much of this book is graced by the thoughts, ideas, and writings of others. It's a synthesis of whatever Art's learned, picked up, or been gifted over the years. He has tried to give credit where credit is due. Any omissions were unintentional.

The library section highlights the authors, programs, and organizations so instrumental in the formation of this book.

Art is also the author of the Amazon #1 bestseller *Get Out Of Your Head, It's A Mess In There.*

Clemmy McWilliam-Le Busque

Clemmy, an artist and author with a rich background in fine arts and a fresh MA in clinical psychology, illustrates the nuanced world of addiction and how it impacts the family.

Her personal journey and professional insights shine through in her second collaboration with friend and colleague Art Dielhenn.

Thanks

Many thanks to all who contributed so much to this book:

Editors:
> Larry Gerber
> Maureen Grady
> Marnae Kelley
> Kat Chezum

Ultimate World Publishing:
> Natasa Denman, Vivienne Mason, Julie Fisher
> Nikola Boskovski & Velin Saramov

E-PR:
> John Steller & Kate Romero

Foreword:
> Dr. Warren "Beau" Christianson
> Director of Aurora Las Encinas Hospital
> Chemical Dependency Services
> Adjunct Professor of Psychiatry USC/Keck Medical School

The Recovery Programs I attend. So much of what I learned working these programs is echoed in these pages.

All those in recovery and life who have shared their experience, strength, and hope.

Library

Alcoholics Anonymous, AA World Services

Twelve Steps and Twelve Traditions, AA World Services

Writing The Big Book, William H. Schaberg

The Little Red Book, Hazelden Foundation

A New Pair of Glasses, Chuck "C"

Drop The Rock, Bill P, Todd W, Sara S.

How Al-Anon Works, Al-Anon Family Groups

Paths to Recovery, Al-Anon Family Groups

One Day at A Time, Al-Anon Family Groups

Opening Our Hearts: Transforming Our Losses, Al-Anon Family Groups

Co-Active Coaching, Whitworth, Kimsey-House and Sandahl

The Coaching Connection, Gorrell and Hoover

Taming Your Gremlin, Rick Carson

A Master Class in Taming Your Gremlin, Rick Carson

Beyond Victim Consciousness, Lynne Forrest

Conjoint Family Therapy, Virginia Satir

ADDICTION IS A FAMILY DISEASE

Introduction to the Family Systems Models,
Richard Schwartz, PhD

Going to Pieces Without Falling Apart, Mark Epstein, MD

The Power of Now, Eckhart Tolle

The New Earth, Eckhart Tolle

Merton's Palace of Nowhere, James Finley

The Contemplative Heart, James Finley

Shift Happens, Robert Holden, PhD

The Untethered Soul, Michael A. Singer

Who Moved My Cheese? Spencer Johnson, MD

The Sermon on the Mount, Emmet Fox

The Tipping Point and *Blink,* Malcolm Gladwell

It's OK That You're Not OK, Megan Devine

Quiet, Susan Cain

Night Falls Fast, Kay Redfield Jamison

On Death and Dying, Elizabeth Kubler-Ross, MD

Self-Matters and Life Strategies, Philip McGraw, PhD

The Subtle Art of Not Giving a Fuck, Mark Manson

Dreams Into Action, Milton Katselas

Practicing the Presence, Joel Goldstein

The Family Crucible, Augustus Y. Napier PhD

You're Not Crazy, Lynn Steinberg PhD

Intimacy Anorexia, Douglas Weiss PhD

Meditation For Beginners, Jack Kornfield

Developing The Leader Within You, John C. Maxwell

The Four Agreements, Don Miguel Ruiz

The Fifth Agreement, Don Miguel and Don Jose Ruiz

Mastery, George Leonard

Excuse Me, Your Life is Waiting, Lynn Grabhorn

Leadership and Self-Deception, Arbinger Institute

The Dark Night of the Soul, Gerald G. May, MD

Breathing Underwater, Richard Roar

The Spirituality of Imperfection, Kurtz and Ketcham

KJV Study Bible, Barbour Publishing

*Any profits
after recouping the costs of producing this book
will be donated to entities dedicated to
those struggling with addiction.*

Notes

ADDICTION IS A FAMILY DISEASE

_____

_____

_____

_____

_____

_____

_____

_____

_____

_____

_____

_____

_____

_____

_____

NOTES

ADDICTION IS A FAMILY DISEASE

_____

_____

_____

_____

_____

_____

_____

_____

_____

_____

_____

_____

_____

_____

_____

NOTES

www.ingramcontent.com/pod-product-compliance
Lightning Source LLC
LaVergne TN
LVHW090445280225
804576LV00004B/15